# DEALING WITH DEBT

*by*
Margaret C. Jasper

Oceana's Legal Almanac Series:
*Law for the Layperson*

Oceana Publications

REF
332.024
JAS

Information contained in this work has been obtained by Oceana Publications from sources believed to be reliable. However, neither the Publisher nor its authors guarantee the accuracy or completeness of any information published herein, and neither the Publisher nor its authors shall be responsible for any errors, omissions or damages arising from the use of this information. This work is published with the understanding that the Publisher and its authors are supplying information, but are not attempting to render legal or other professional services. If such services are required, the assistance of an appropriate professional should be sought.

You may order this or any other Oxford University Press publication by visiting the Oxford University Press and Oceana websites at www.oup.com and www.oceanalaw.com respectively.

Library of Congress Control Number: 2006935508

ISBN 0-19-532363-7
ISBN 978-0-19-532363-4

Oceana's Legal Almanac Series: Law for the Layperson
ISSN 1075-7376

©2007 Oxford University Press, Inc.

All rights reserved. No part of this publication may be reproduced or transmitted in any form or by any means, electronic or mechanical, including photocopy, recording, xerography, or any information storage and retrieval system, without permission in writing from the publisher.

Manufactured in the United States of America on acid-free paper.

To My Husband Chris

Your love and support
are my motivation and inspiration

-and-

In memory of my son, Jimmy

# Table of Contents

ABOUT THE AUTHOR .............................................. vii
INTRODUCTION ................................................. xi

### CHAPTER 1:
### WHAT IS DEBT?
IN GENERAL ...................................................... 1
DEBT CLASSIFICATION ............................................ 1
   Secured Debts ................................................ 1
   Unsecured Debts ............................................. 4
   Joint Debts ................................................... 4
TYPES OF CREDIT ................................................ 5
CREDIT CARD DEBT .............................................. 6
HOW IS THE INTEREST RATE CALCULATED? ......................... 6
   Simple Interest Rate .......................................... 6
   Periodic Interest Rate ......................................... 6
   Annual Percentage Rate ....................................... 6
   The Federal Reserve .......................................... 7
   Usury Laws ................................................... 7

### CHAPTER 2:
### DEBT MANAGEMENT
UNDERSTANDING YOUR FINANCIAL SITUATION ...................... 9
   Personal Net Worth ........................................... 9
   Cash Flow .................................................... 9
GETTING RID OF BAD DEBT ...................................... 11
START WITH A PLAN ............................................ 11
ESTABLISH A PERSONAL BUDGET ................................ 12
CREDIT COUNSELING ............................................ 13
HOUSING COUNSELING AGENCIES ............................... 14
DEBT CONSOLIDATION .......................................... 14
   Consolidating Student Loans .................................. 14
   Debt Consolidation Advertisements ............................ 14

## CHAPTER 3:
## TAX DEBTS

INCOME TAXES .................................................. 15
INTERNAL REVENUE SERVICE TAX COLLECTION ...................... 15
   The Tax Bill ................................................ 15
   Interest and Penalties ...................................... 16
   Installment Agreements ..................................... 17
   Offer in Compromise ........................................ 18
TAX COLLECTION PROCEDURES ..................................... 19
   Federal Tax Lien ........................................... 19
   Release of Notice of Federal Tax Lien ...................... 20
   Filing an Appeal ........................................... 20
   Federal Tax Levy ........................................... 21
   Tax Sale ................................................... 23
   Filing an Appeal ........................................... 24
   IRS Taxpayer Advocate Program .............................. 25
PROPERTY TAXES ................................................ 25

## CHAPTER 4:
## THE DEBT COLLECTION PROCESS

IN GENERAL .................................................... 27
INTERNAL DEBT COLLECTION DEPARTMENTS .......................... 27
INDEPENDENT DEBT COLLECTION AGENCIES .......................... 29
NONJUDICIAL DEBT COLLECTION ................................... 31
   Compromise and Settlement .................................. 31
   Arbitration and Mediation .................................. 31
   Confession of Judgment ..................................... 32
JUDICIAL DEBT COLLECTION ...................................... 32
   Statute of Limitations ..................................... 32
   The Litigation Process ..................................... 32

## CHAPTER 5:
## DEBT COLLECTION HARASSMENT

IN GENERAL .................................................... 35
ALTERNATIVES TO LITIGATION .................................... 35
GATHERING EVIDENCE ............................................ 36
COMMON LAW THEORIES OF RECOVERY ............................... 37
   Intentional Infliction of Emotional Distress ............... 37
   Intentional Interference with Business Relationships ....... 38
   Miscellaneous Common Law Theories of Recovery .............. 38
ASSESSING DAMAGES ............................................. 38
CAUSATION ..................................................... 38

THE FAIR DEBT COLLECTION PRACTICES ACT . . . . . . . . . . . . . . . . . . . . . . . 39
   In General . . . . . . . . . . . . . . . . . . . . . . . . . . . . . . . . . . . . . . . . . . . . . . . . 39
   Obligations of Debt Collectors. . . . . . . . . . . . . . . . . . . . . . . . . . . . . . . . . 39
   Prohibited Practices . . . . . . . . . . . . . . . . . . . . . . . . . . . . . . . . . . . . . . . . 40
   Remedies. . . . . . . . . . . . . . . . . . . . . . . . . . . . . . . . . . . . . . . . . . . . . . . . . 41

## CHAPTER 6:
## JUDGMENT ENFORCEMENT

IN GENERAL . . . . . . . . . . . . . . . . . . . . . . . . . . . . . . . . . . . . . . . . . . . . . . . . 43
THE JUDGMENT PROOF DEBTOR. . . . . . . . . . . . . . . . . . . . . . . . . . . . . . . . 43
FINANCIAL DISCLOSURE. . . . . . . . . . . . . . . . . . . . . . . . . . . . . . . . . . . . . . 44
RESTRAINING NOTICE . . . . . . . . . . . . . . . . . . . . . . . . . . . . . . . . . . . . . . . 44
METHODS OF JUDGMENT ENFORCEMENT. . . . . . . . . . . . . . . . . . . . . . . . . 44
   In General . . . . . . . . . . . . . . . . . . . . . . . . . . . . . . . . . . . . . . . . . . . . . . . . 44
   Attachment and Garnishment. . . . . . . . . . . . . . . . . . . . . . . . . . . . . . . . . 45
   Wage Garnishment . . . . . . . . . . . . . . . . . . . . . . . . . . . . . . . . . . . . . . . . . 46
   Bank Execution . . . . . . . . . . . . . . . . . . . . . . . . . . . . . . . . . . . . . . . . . . . . 46
   Property Execution . . . . . . . . . . . . . . . . . . . . . . . . . . . . . . . . . . . . . . . . . 47
   Real Property Execution . . . . . . . . . . . . . . . . . . . . . . . . . . . . . . . . . . . . . 47
   Statutory Exemptions . . . . . . . . . . . . . . . . . . . . . . . . . . . . . . . . . . . . . . . 48
   Satisfaction of Judgment and Release of Lien. . . . . . . . . . . . . . . . . . . . . 48
WRONGFUL ATTACHMENT OR GARNISHMENT. . . . . . . . . . . . . . . . . . . . . 48
   Malicious Prosecution Action . . . . . . . . . . . . . . . . . . . . . . . . . . . . . . . . . 48
   Liability on the Attachment or Garnishment Bond. . . . . . . . . . . . . . . . . 49
   Abuse of Process Actions . . . . . . . . . . . . . . . . . . . . . . . . . . . . . . . . . . . . 49
   Damages . . . . . . . . . . . . . . . . . . . . . . . . . . . . . . . . . . . . . . . . . . . . . . . . . 49
SECURED TRANSACTIONS. . . . . . . . . . . . . . . . . . . . . . . . . . . . . . . . . . . . . 50
   In General . . . . . . . . . . . . . . . . . . . . . . . . . . . . . . . . . . . . . . . . . . . . . . . . 50
   The Security Agreement . . . . . . . . . . . . . . . . . . . . . . . . . . . . . . . . . . . . . 50
   Risk of Loss . . . . . . . . . . . . . . . . . . . . . . . . . . . . . . . . . . . . . . . . . . . . . . . 51
   Default. . . . . . . . . . . . . . . . . . . . . . . . . . . . . . . . . . . . . . . . . . . . . . . . . . . 51
   Redemption . . . . . . . . . . . . . . . . . . . . . . . . . . . . . . . . . . . . . . . . . . . . . . 51

## CHAPTER 7:
## CONSUMER BANKRUPTCY

IN GENERAL . . . . . . . . . . . . . . . . . . . . . . . . . . . . . . . . . . . . . . . . . . . . . . . . 53
EXPLORING THE ALTERNATIVES . . . . . . . . . . . . . . . . . . . . . . . . . . . . . . . . 53
ADVANTAGES AND DISADVANTAGES OF FILING BANKRUPTCY . . . . . . . . . . . . 55
COMMENCING THE BANKRUPTCY CASE. . . . . . . . . . . . . . . . . . . . . . . . . . 56
   Chapter 13–Individual Debt Adjustment . . . . . . . . . . . . . . . . . . . . . . . . 57
   Chapter 7–Liquidation . . . . . . . . . . . . . . . . . . . . . . . . . . . . . . . . . . . . . . 58
   The Automatic Stay . . . . . . . . . . . . . . . . . . . . . . . . . . . . . . . . . . . . . . . . 60
   Discharged Debts. . . . . . . . . . . . . . . . . . . . . . . . . . . . . . . . . . . . . . . . . . 62

## CHAPTER 8:
## REHABILITATING YOUR CREDIT

WHAT IS A CREDIT REPORT? ........................................... 67
REQUESTING YOUR CREDIT REPORT................................ 67
    The FACT Act .................................................................. 68
MONITOR YOUR CREDIT REPORT REGULARLY ..................... 69
    The *Fair Credit Reporting Act*............................................ 70
    Identify Problems ............................................................ 71
    Dispute Erroneous Information ........................................ 71
    Inquiries ........................................................................ 72
    Early Warning Notice...................................................... 72
HOW LONG DOES NEGATIVE INFORMATION REMAIN IN A CREDIT
REPORT?...................................................................... 72
    Bankruptcy..................................................................... 73
    Charged Off Accounts..................................................... 73
    Closed Accounts ............................................................. 73
    Collection Accounts ........................................................ 73
    Inquiries ........................................................................ 73
    Judgments ..................................................................... 73
    Late Payments ............................................................... 73
    Tax Liens ....................................................................... 73
OBTAINING LEGAL SERVICES ........................................... 73
CREDIT REPAIR SERVICES ............................................... 74
    The Credit Repair Organizations Act................................. 75

## APPENDICES

APPENDIX 1: TABLE OF THE MOST COMMON FORECLOSURE METHODS,
BY STATE .................................................................... 77
APPENDIX 2: TABLE OF STATE USURY LAWS ........................ 79
APPENDIX 3: INSTALLMENT AGREEMENT REQUEST .................... 83
APPENDIX 4: TABLE OF STATE STATUTES GOVERNING DEBT
COLLECTION................................................................. 87
APPENDIX 5: CREDITOR DEMAND LETTER ........................... 89
APPENDIX 6: PAYMENT AGREEMENT CONFIRMATION LETTER........... 91
APPENDIX 7: NOTICE TO COLLECTION AGENCY TO CEASE CONTACT ...... 93
APPENDIX 8: AGREEMENT TO COMPROMISE A DEBT ................... 95
APPENDIX 9: FTC CONSUMER COMPLAINT FORM ..................... 97
APPENDIX 10: CREDIT CARD ISSUER ITEM DISPUTE LETTER .......... 103
APPENDIX 11: FAIR DEBT COLLECTION PRACTICES ACT.............. 105
APPENDIX 12: DEBT COLLECTION HARASSMENT COMPLAINT .......... 119
APPENDIX 13: SATISFACTION OF JUDGMENT AND RELEASE OF LIEN..... 123

APPENDIX 14: DEBTOR'S VOLUNTARY BANKRUPTCY PETITION
(OFFICIAL FORM 1) ............................................. 125
APPENDIX 15: CHAPTER 13 REPAYMENT PLAN ...................... 129
APPENDIX 16: FEDERAL EXEMPTIONS UNDER §522(D) OF THE
BANKRUPTCY CODE ............................................. 137
APPENDIX 17: TABLE OF STATE STATUTES GOVERNING BANKRUPTCY
EXEMPTIONS................................................... 139
APPENDIX 18: PROOF OF CLAIM ................................. 143
APPENDIX 19: REAFFIRMATION AGREEMENT ....................... 145
APPENDIX 20: BANKRUPTCY DISCHARGE ORDER .................... 155
APPENDIX 21: DIRECTORY OF UNITED STATES BANKRUPTCY COURTS
MAIN OFFICES................................................. 157
APPENDIX 22: DISCLOSURE FEES UNDER THE FAIR AND ACCURATE
CREDIT TRANSACTIONS (FACT) ACT .............................. 165
APPENDIX 23: CREDIT REPORTING AGENCY INFORMATION
DISPUTE LETTER .............................................. 169
APPENDIX 24: CREDIT REPORT CHECKLIST ....................... 171
APPENDIX 25: THE CREDIT REPAIR ORGANIZATIONS ACT ........... 177

GLOSSARY..................................................... 187
BIBLIOGRAPHY AND ADDITIONAL READING ........................ 201

# ABOUT THE AUTHOR

MARGARET C. JASPER is an attorney engaged in the general practice of law in South Salem, New York, concentrating in the areas of personal injury and entertainment law. Ms. Jasper holds a Juris Doctor degree from Pace University School of Law, White Plains, New York, is a member of the New York and Connecticut bars, and is certified to practice before the United States District Courts for the Southern and Eastern Districts of New York, the United States Court of Appeals for the Second Circuit, and the United States Supreme Court.

Ms. Jasper has been appointed to the law guardian panel for the Family Court of the State of New York, is a member of a number of professional organizations and associations, and is a New York State licensed real estate broker operating as Jasper Real Estate, in South Salem, New York.

Margaret Jasper maintains a website at http://www.JasperLawOffice.com.

In 2004, Ms. Jasper successfully argued a case before the New York Court of Appeals, which gives mothers of babies who are stillborn due to medical negligence the right to bring a legal action and recover emotional distress damages. This successful appeal overturned a 26-year old New York case precedent, which previously prevented mothers of stillborn babies from suing their negligent medical providers.

Ms. Jasper is the author and general editor of the following legal almanacs:

> AIDS Law
> The Americans with Disabilities Act
> Animal Rights Law
> Auto Leasing
> Bankruptcy Law for the Individual Debtor
> Banks and their Customers
> Becoming a Citizen

## ABOUT THE AUTHOR

Buying and Selling Your Home
Commercial Law
Consumer Rights Law
Co-ops and Condominiums: Your Rights and Obligations As Owner
Copyright Law
Credit Cards and the Law
Custodial Rights
Dealing with Debt
Dictionary of Selected Legal Terms
Drunk Driving Law
DWI, DUI and the Law
Education Law
Elder Law
Employee Rights in the Workplace
Employment Discrimination Under Title VII
Environmental Law
Estate Planning
Everyday Legal Forms
Executors and Personal Representatives: Rights and Responsibilities
Harassment in the Workplace
Health Care and Your Rights
Hiring Household Help and Contractors: Your Rights and Obligations Under the Law
Home Mortgage Law Primer
Hospital Liability Law
How To Change Your Name
How To Protect Your Challenged Child
How To Start Your Own Business
Identity Theft and How To Protect Yourself
Individual Bankruptcy and Restructuring
Injured on the Job: Employee Rights, Worker's Compensation and Disability Insurance Law
International Adoption
Juvenile Justice and Children's Law
Labor Law
Landlord-Tenant Law
Law for the Small Business Owner
The Law of Attachment and Garnishment
The Law of Buying and Selling
The Law of Capital Punishment
The Law of Child Custody
The Law of Contracts
The Law of Debt Collection

The Law of Dispute Resolution
The Law of Immigration
The Law of Libel and Slander
The Law of Medical Malpractice
The Law of No-Fault Insurance
The Law of Obscenity and Pornography
The Law of Personal Injury
The Law of Premises Liability
The Law of Product Liability
The Law of Speech and the First Amendment
The Law of Violence Against Women
Lemon Laws
Living Together: Practical Legal Issues
Living Wills
Marriage and Divorce
Missing and Exploited Children: How to Protect Your Child
Motor Vehicle Law
Nursing Home Negligence
Patent Law
Pet Law
Prescription Drugs
Privacy and the Internet: Your Rights and Expectations Under the Law
Probate Law
Real Estate Law for the Homeowner and Broker
Religion and the Law
Retirement Planning
The Right to Die
Rights of Single Parents
Small Claims Court
Social Security Law
Special Education Law
Teenagers and Substance Abuse
Trademark Law
Trouble Next Door: What to do With Your Neighbor
Victim's Rights Law
Welfare: Your Rights and the Law
What if It Happened to You: Violent Crimes and Victims' Rights
What if the Product Doesn't Work: Warranties & Guarantees
Workers' Compensation Law
Your Child's Legal Rights: An Overview
Your Rights in a Class Action Suit
Your Rights as a Tenant
Your Rights Under the Family and Medical Leave Act
You've Been Fired: Your Rights and Remedies

# INTRODUCTION

Debt comes in many forms, including but not limited to credit card debt, mortgages, home equity loans, car loans, consumer loans, student loans, and taxes. Many people trying to balance large amounts of debt with incomes that have failed to keep pace are barely making ends meet. It is often a very delicate balance. An individual in this situation, who is confronted with an unexpected crisis, such as illness or loss of employment, suddenly finds their income reduced to the point where he or she is no longer able to pay their bills. Debts have to be prioritized, with rent or mortgage payments and utility bills of paramount concern.

Meanwhile, the stack of credit card bills, loan payments, and automobile notes builds. Late fees, overdue fees, and skyrocketing credit card interest rates make it almost impossible to get out from under this mounting debt. Then, to make matters worse, the threatening and intimidating debt collection letters and phone calls begin, and the debtor is faced with repossession, foreclosure and forced to consider filing for bankruptcy to stop the debt collection process.

This almanac sets forth an overview of the various types of debt facing consumers today, the manner in which different categories of debt are treated and ways a consumer can manage their debt and solve their financial problems without having to resort to drastic measures, such as bankruptcy. The almanac also discusses debt consolidation and credit counseling, and advises the consumer on how to negotiate directly with creditors and tax collectors regarding outstanding debt before the debt collection process begins.

The debt collection process and an overview of the law applicable to debt collection is also explored, as well as what the debtor may expect to happen when debts go unpaid. including judgments, wage garnishment, repossession, and foreclosure. This almanac also discusses the state and federal laws designed to protect the debtor from harassment,

## INTRODUCTION

threats and other illegal tactics used by those seeking to collect on a debt.

Scenarios where bankruptcy may be the preferred route once all other options have been considered are also presented, including an overview of the new rules governing consumer bankruptcies that took effect pursuant to the *Bankruptcy Abuse Prevention and Consumer Protection Act of 2005*. Finally, this almanac discusses credit rehabilitation, and ways in which a debtor can begin to repair their damaged credit rating once they have been able to resolve their financial problems.

The Appendix provides applicable statutes, sample forms, and other pertinent information and data. The Glossary contains definitions of many of the terms used throughout the almanac.

# CHAPTER 1: WHAT IS DEBT?

## IN GENERAL

A debt is generally defined as an obligation or liability to pay. A debtor is one who owes a monetary debt to another, known as a creditor. There is no shortage of debtors in the United States. Statistics demonstrate that Americans have gone credit crazy. Consumer debt is at an all time high. More people are spending now than ever before, and less are saving. It seems that credit is available to anyone these days, regardless of his or her negative credit rating or lack of income. However, it comes at a very costly price, as interest rates can go as high as thirty percent or more, with additional fees and penalties tacked on for late payments, exceeding the credit limit, annual fees, etc. The result is that the average consumer can never pay off the principal balance, especially if he or she sticks to the minimum payment requested, keeping them forever in debt.

## DEBT CLASSIFICATION

Debts may be classified according to certain factors, such as the type of lender and the rights the lender retains according to their agreement with the borrower, as set forth below.

### Secured Debts

A debt is "secured" if the lender, by agreement, has retained some kind of interest in the borrower's property in return for making the loan. Secured debts usually involve large purchases, such as homes, automobiles, appliances and furniture. This security interest gives the lender some assurance that the debt will be repaid, or that the lender will not suffer a total loss if the borrower defaults, because the secured item can be repossessed.

A secured debt would also arise if an individual seeking to borrow

# WHAT IS DEBT?

money from a lending institution, such as a bank or finance company, is required by the lender to pledge some item of value as collateral for the loan, such as jewelry or a car. The loan is secured by the collateral; even though the collateral has nothing to do with the reason the individual borrowed the money in the first place.

A security interest also provides the secured party with the assurance that if the debtor files bankruptcy, the lender may be able to recover the value of the loan by taking possession of the collateral, instead of receiving only a fraction of the borrower's property after it is divided among all creditors, or nothing at all.

Most consumers are concerned with protecting their two most valuable assets: their home and their car. An overview of the laws concerning home foreclosure and automobile repossession is discussed below.

### Home Foreclosure

If you default on your home loan payments, your lender will seek to foreclose on your loan and sell your home. Depending on the state, the available methods of foreclosure may be judicial, nonjudicial or both. A judicial foreclosure requires the lender to file a formal complaint against you in court. You are then afforded an opportunity to answer the complaint and present a defense to the foreclosure action. If the lender wins and obtains a judgment of foreclosure, a sale will be scheduled. You are generally allowed to stop the foreclosure sale at any time up until the time of sale by paying the lender all amounts due, including attorney fees and costs associated with the foreclosure.

A nonjudicial foreclosure sale occurs when a mortgage or deed of trust contains a Power of Sale clause, allowing the lender to pursue foreclosure if you default on your home loan. The lender does not have to obtain a court order to proceed with a sale of your home. Typically, the lender will file a Notice of Default with the county clerk's office governing the location of the property. The lender is usually required to send a copy of the Notice of Default to the homeowner and to any other entity holding a lien on the property. The Notice of Default identifies the property and the amount owed, and gives the homeowner a certain amount of time to pay the debt or a foreclosure sale is scheduled.

The lender is generally required to inform the public of the impending foreclosure sale. Depending on the state, the required notice may be made by publishing a Notice of Sale in a local newspaper or posting the Notice of Sale at the courthouse or other public venue. The Notice of Sale must contain the date, time, location, and terms of the sale. Most foreclosure sales are conducted like a public auction, with the property going to the highest bidder, who is issued a deed to the property upon payment of the bid amount.

Some states provide for a redemption period following the sale. During the redemption period—e.g., one year—the homeowner has the right to redeem the property. Other states do not allow for redemption, and once sold, you can never get the property back.

A table setting forth the most common method of foreclosure, by state, is set forth at Appendix 1 of this almanac.

### Automobile Repossession

A common type of secured debt is an automobile loan. The automobile finance company retains a security interest in the car. Thus, it is legal for the lender to repossess an automobile when the debtor defaults on the payments. They commonly do so without notification. The lender usually hires someone to track down the car and simply take it by whatever means possible, e.g. tow it, hot wire it, etc. That person is commonly referred to as the "repo man." He or she will use personal information, such as the debtor's home or workplace address, to find the car. However, the law usually doesn't allow your lender to commit a breach of the peace in connection with repossession.

If you are concerned that your car may be repossessed before you are able to catch up on your payments, don't leave it out in the open where it can easily be found. A garaged car is usually safe because the "repo" agent is not legally permitted to break into your garage. In some states, removing your car from a closed garage without your permission may constitute a breach of the peace. Lenders who breach the peace in seizing your car may be required to compensate you if they harm you or your property.

If, however, you find that your car has been repossessed, it is important to seek to reinstate the contract as soon as possible. The debtor can generally obtain the vehicle and reinstate the contract once all of the arrears, and any expenses incurred by the lender as a result of the repossession, are paid in full. The lender will usually try and sell the car if the debtor fails to reinstate the contract in a timely manner. Some state laws limit the ways a lender can repossess and sell a vehicle to reduce or eliminate your debt. If any rules are violated, the lender may be required to pay you damages.

Depending on the law of the state in which you reside, the lender is generally required to give the debtor notice prior to the sale. If the contract is not reinstated within the time period required by law, the car will be sold. Unfortunately, the lender usually does not make an effort to sell the car for its retail value; therefore, you will still be liable for any deficiency between the sale price and the amount you still owe on the vehicle.

For example, if the balance on your car loan is $7,000, and the lender sells your car for $4,000, you will still be liable to the lender for the difference of $3,000 plus costs and legal fees.

Depending on your state's law and other factors, if you are sued for a deficiency judgment, you should be notified of the date of the court hearing. This may be your only opportunity to present any legal defense. If the lender breached the peace when seizing the vehicle or failed to sell the car in a commercially reasonable manner, you may have a legal defense against a deficiency judgment.

It is always preferable to try and prevent your vehicle from being repossessed than disputing the repossession after it has occurred. You should contact your lender as soon as you believe you will be late with your loan payment. Many lenders will try to work out a solution. For example, you may be able to negotiate a delay in your payment or a revised schedule of payments. However, if you reach an agreement to modify your original contract, get it in writing to avoid questions later.

If your lender refuses to accept a late payment or revise your contract, and you are certain that you are facing repossession, you may voluntarily agree to repossession. This reduces the lender's costs, which you would be responsible for if the lender was forced to repossess the car. However, even if you return the car voluntarily, you are responsible for paying any deficiency on your contract, and your lender may still report the late payments and/or repossession to the credit reporting agencies.

The reader is advised to check the law of the state in which he or she lives on the specific rights afforded a consumer whose motor vehicle has been repossessed.

### Unsecured Debts

Unsecured debts are those for which the lender has retained no interest in any of the items purchased and has not required the debtor to put up any collateral to secure the loan. Thus, if the debtor defaults on the payments, the lender has no legal right to repossess any of the goods or collateral. Unsecured debts are the most common type of consumer debt, and may include credit card debt and uncollateralized loans.

### Joint Debts

Two or more people may incur joint debts. This situation usually occurs when an individual guarantees—i.e., co-signs—on another party's loan so that the borrower is approved. For example, a parent may co-sign for his or her child's automobile loan. If the original party defaults, the creditor will look to the co-signer for payments. Generally, the co-signer is as equally liable for the debt as the defaulting party.

Another scenario in which a third party may become obligated on another's loan is when the third party agrees, after the fact, to assume the original debtor's obligation. Again, both the original debtor and the party assuming the obligation are equally liable to the creditor for the debt.

Spouses commonly incur joint debts. For example, a husband and wife may jointly apply for a credit card. If one spouse uses the credit line, and then defaults on the payments, the other spouse is still liable, whether or not he or she incurred the debt. Joint debts often raise problems following a divorce.

For example, although the parties may agree that one spouse will pay the credit card payments, if he or she reneges, the other spouse is still liable for the debt. The innocent spouse's only recourse would be to make the payments to avoid damage to his or her credit rating, and then sue the non-paying spouse for breach of the agreement. This can be expensive, time-consuming, and fruitless if the non-paying spouse is judgment proof.

**TYPES OF CREDIT**

The two major types of credit are open-end and closed-end credit. Open-end credit—e.g., credit cards and home equity lines of credit—is also called revolving credit because it allows you to borrow up to an authorized amount—i.e., your credit limit—on a continuous basis.

If you open a credit card account, the credit card issuer will authorize a certain credit limit. If you are trying to establish credit, your initial credit limit will probably be small—e.g., $300. If you make timely payments, your credit limit may gradually increase. The difference between your credit limit and your outstanding charges is called your available credit. As you incur additional charges, your available credit is reduced. When you make payments, your available credit is replenished.

Home equity and personal lines of credit are similar to credit cards. The difference between the two is that a home equity line of credit is secured by the equity in your home whereas a personal line of credit is unsecured. As with credit cards, a line of credit allows you to withdraw funds up to the authorized limit and, as you pay down the balance, the available credit line increases.

## WHAT IS DEBT?

**CREDIT CARD DEBT**

Over the past 25 years, credit card debt has more than tripled, from approximately $238 billion in 1990 to $755 billion in 2004. The average American household now has approximately $7,300 of credit card debt, and the average credit card interest rate is 16.75%. At this rate, it could take 44 years to pay off this credit card debt and cost the consumer over $16,000 in interest if he or she continued to pay the minimum payment due, which many consumers choose to do. Fortunately, 42% credit card holders now pay off their balances in full each month, thus avoiding interest. Of course, credit card issuers are not happy when a credit card balance is paid off in full because it cuts into their profits.

Recognizing that paying the minimum payment requested on a credit card keeps the consumer indebted for many years, the Office of the Comptroller of Currency (OCC) instituted new rules regarding minimum credit card payments. The new rules went into full effect in 2005. Under the new rules, the minimum monthly payment amount for a credit card increased from 2% to 4% or more, depending on the bank that issued the credit card.

The minimum payment increase has been met with mixed reviews. Some consumers are unhappy that they have to increase their limited budget for credit card payments while others recognize that raising the minimum payment will help them pay down their debt much sooner.

**HOW IS THE INTEREST RATE CALCULATED?**

### Simple Interest Rate

When you borrow money, you pay an interest rate on the loan. The interest rate is stated as a yearly percentage rate—the interest cost of borrowing for one year. For example, if you borrow $100,000 at an interest rate of 10%, the interest for one year costs $10,000.

### Periodic Interest Rate

The periodic interest rate is the interest rate you pay for a period of time less than one year, and it is calculated in a similar manner as simple interest. For example, if you borrow $100,000 at an interest rate of 10%, you would divide the annual interest rate by the number of periods. Thus, if the period is one month, you would multiply $100,000 by 10% by 1/12 ($833.33).

### Annual Percentage Rate

The annual percentage rate (APR)—also called the effective interest rate or the compounded interest rate—is the real rate of interest you pay on a loan. The APR is calculated by including any of the closing costs you pay on your loan. For example, if you borrow $100,000 and pay $10,000 in closing costs, you "effectively" borrow $90,000, provided you pay the closing costs at closing instead of rolling them into your loan.

### The Federal Reserve

The Federal Reserve is the central bank of the United States. The Federal Reserve evaluates the state of the economy in determining future interest rates. If it appears that the economy is slowing down, the Federal Reserve will lower interest rates in order to stimulate the economy, whereas if it anticipates too much growth or the possibility of inflation, interest rates may be raised. Thus, the action the Federal Reserve takes in lowering or raising the interest rates willl affect the payment amount on any adjustable note loan you may have accordingly.

### Usury Laws

Many state laws provide that an individual cannot lend money at an interest rate that exceeds the state's statutory maximum—i.e., "the usury limit." "Usury" is generally defined as charging a price for credit that exceeds the usury limits set by law. Some states have no established usury limit. In addition, there are presently no federal usury limits. The federal government relies on the Truth in Lending Act, which guarantees that lenders disclose their rates, fees and terms.

You may notice that your state has a reasonable usury limit, such as 12%, but your credit card carries an interest rate of 25%. The reason for this huge gap in permissible interest is that the interest rate assessed on your credit card is that of the state in which the bank's credit card operations are situated. As long as the credit card issuer abides by the law of the state in which their credit card operations are located, the interest rates and fees they assess are legal, even if the consumer lives in a state that has a much lower usury limit. Most credit card issuers move their operations to the states that have these lender-friendly interest caps and few restrictions.

Therefore, it is advisable to take notice of the state in which the credit card operations for your credit cards are located, as this may indicate how high your credit card interest rates may rise, particularly if you make a late payment or otherwise default on your credit card agreement. Generally, credit card issuers include a provision in the credit agreement that allows them to raise your interest rate to their highest "default" rate if you fail to abide by any of the credit card terms, e.g., by exceeding your credit limit or making a late payment.

## WHAT IS DEBT?

Presently, there are 26 states that have no limit on what bank credit card issuers can charge for interest rates, and 27 states have no limit on what they can charge for annual fees. California, Delaware, South Dakota and Tennessee have no set maximums on what they can charge for delinquency fees, cash advance fees, overlimit fees, transaction fees, ATM fees, etc., and do not provide any type of grace period. It is no coincidence that many credit cards are issued under the laws of those four states.

A table of state usury laws is set forth at Appendix 2 of this almanac.

# CHAPTER 2: DEBT MANAGEMENT

## UNDERSTANDING YOUR FINANCIAL SITUATION

### Personal Net Worth

Your personal net worth is the difference between your personal assets and personal liabilities. Your personal assets include the value of your home and any other real property you own; your car; your investments, including stocks, bonds, money market funds, certificates of deposit; the funds in your savings and checking accounts; and the value of any other assets you own. Your personal liabilities include the mortgage on your home, your debts, such as your auto loan and your credit card debt.

As the recent boom in the housing industry demonstrated, your personal net worth can change drastically depending on the marketplace. Many homes doubled and tripled in value in the last five years, thus, the homeowner's personal net worth increased accordingly. Incurring large amounts of credit card debt will decrease your personal net worth. If you invest heavily in the stock market, your personal net worth rises and falls on a daily basis

Your personal net worth is an important factor in the credit approval process. Credit applications generally contain columns for you to fill in your assets and liabilities. The lender uses this information to determine your net worth and thus your ability to pay off the debt.

### Cash Flow

Your cash flow is the difference between your cash inflow and cash outflow. You can calculate your monthly cash flow by totaling your income for the month and deducting your monthly bills. Your cash inflow should include your net wages and other income that you regularly take in as cash each month. Do not include any amounts that are not

## DEBT MANAGEMENT

received on regular basis, such as your yearly tax refund or bonus from your employer.

EXAMPLE

| Net wages: | $2,000 |
|---|---|
| Interest income: | $50 |
| Part-time job: | $300 |
| Total Cash Inflow: | $2,350 |

Your cash outflow would include all of the bills you pay on a regular basis, such as your mortgage note or rent, car payment, credit card and loan payments, utilities, food, gas, etc.

EXAMPLE:

| Rent: | $750 |
|---|---|
| Car lease payment: | $150 |
| Utilities: | $200 |
| Food: | $250 |
| Credit card payments: | $100 |
| Transportation: | $100 |
| Total Cash Outflow: | $1,550 |

The difference between your monthly cash inflow and cash outflow is your personal net cash flow.

EXAMPLE:

| Total Cash Inflow: | $2,350 |
|---|---|
| Less Total Cash Outflow: | $1,550 |
| Monthly Cash Flow: | $800 |

Your monthly cash flow is the amount you have left to save and/or invest. By putting these calculations on paper, you can see where your money is going, and whether or not you can improve your cash flow by increasing your cash inflows and decreasing your cash outflows.

For example, if you have a home mortgage, you can try to protect your cash flow due to fluctuations in interest rates by selecting the appropriate loan for the situation. A fixed-rate loan locks in your interest rate, thus your monthly payment will stay the same despite rising interest rates, and your cash flow will not be impacted. If interest rates are declining, an adjustable rate mortgage will lower your monthly loan payments, thus increasing your cash flow.

## GETTING RID OF BAD DEBT

In order to effectively deal with your debt problems, it is important to distinguish between good and bad debt. Credit cards and loans that have high interest rates—i.e., 10% or higher—definitely fall under the "bad debt" column. A low interest mortgage loan is generally considered "good debt." The interest you pay is tax deductible, and the value of real estate is certain to increase over time. In addition, you continue to build equity in your home as you make the principal payments on your loan.

If you carry a lot of bad debt, you should try and pay off these balances as soon as possible, even before you put money away for various savings plans or retirement. It doesn't make sense to put money in a savings account that earns 4% interest, when you continue to pay credit card payments on a credit card that has a 21% interest rate.

To figure out which creditors to get rid of first, make a list of all your debts according to their interest rates. Pay off the debts that have the highest interest rate first, particularly credit card debts. If necessary, it is advisable to use your savings to pay off these high interest debts as you will be able to save much more once these debts are paid.

## START WITH A PLAN

Although being in debt may be unpleasant and embarrassing, the problem can be managed. The first step in effectively managing your debts is to examine your financial circumstances, as follows:

1. List all sources of monthly income, including such items as wages, pensions, social security, interest income, and child support.

2. List all of your necessary monthly expenses, including such items as food, clothing, housing, utilities, transportation costs, and medical expenses.

3. List all other monthly debts. Prioritize the debts according to their importance, balance, and overdue status, so as to eliminate or reduce any overlimit and/or past due fees that may be assessed against you.

4. Deduct the total necessary monthly expenses (Item #2) from the total monthly income (Item #1). If there is a balance left over, this would be the amount available to make payments on some of the other monthly debts (Item #3).

5. If there is not enough money left over to make all monthly payments, make payments according to the priorities set forth. For example, if the car payment is two months past due and subject to

repossession, don't send a check to the "book of the month" club. In short, don't make payments on low priority bills, despite the pressure you may get from a collection agency.

6. If there is no money left over after paying the essentials, or if the debts are so overwhelming that it is unlikely they will ever be repaid in full, do not ignore the problem but consider your alternatives, as more fully discussed in this almanac.

### ESTABLISH A PERSONAL BUDGET

Establishing a personal budget is helpful in controlling your personal expenses and developing the discipline to save. When establishing a budget, you should start by setting spending limits that will help keep you within your means of paying your bills. Generally, a monthly budget is preferable insofar as most bills are paid on a monthly basis. Keep detailed accurate records of your monthly expenses so you can compare your actual budget to your proposed budget. Review your actual and proposed budgets carefully to identify positive variances in the two budgets—i.e., when your actual cash outflow is less than your budgeted cash outflow—to determine how much you may be able to save or invest.

EXAMPLE:

| | |
|---|---|
| Budgeted cash outflow: | $2,500 |
| Actual cash outflow: | $2,250 |
| Positive Variance: | $250 |

Using the above example, you would have an extra two hundred fifty ($250) dollars in your budget that you can use to save or invest. Your first priority for saving is an emergency fund in case of a medical emergency, employment lay-off or other unexpected financial problem. Your target emergency fund should consist of funds that can cover three to six months of your budgeted expenses, and should only be used for that purpose.

If you plan to invest your emergency fund, you should make sure you will have immediate access to the cash if the need arises. Thus, your funds should be placed in a safe, very liquid investment that also earns you interest, e.g., apportioned in short-term certificates of deposit that have staggered maturity dates. You should also keep a portion of those funds in a savings account for immediate access in case of an emergency.

## CREDIT COUNSELING

If you need help in dealing with your credit or lease contract, consider using a credit counseling service. There are nonprofit organizations in every state that advise consumers on debt management. There are also a number of for-profit companies that "claim" to offer free or low-cost credit counseling services; therefore, it is important to do a background check on a company before making an appointment.

A legitimate credit counseling service is generally a nonprofit organization that employs counselors who are knowledgeable about credit and debt collection, who offer their counseling services at little or no cost to consumers. Credit counseling agencies may also offer educational materials and workshops. In addition, universities, military bases, credit unions, and housing authorities often operate nonprofit counseling programs. You should also check with your local bank or consumer protection office to see if it has a list of reputable, low-cost financial counseling services.

The credit counselor acts as an intermediary between the creditor and debtor. The credit counselor helps the debtor prepare a debt repayment plan that is acceptable to both debtor and creditor that pays the debts over a period of time. The counselor is usually able to get the creditor to waive finance and late payment charges so that the debtor need only repay the principal balance due. Once a budget has been established, the debtor generally pays one monthly payment to the service, which apportions the money among the creditors until the debts are paid in full, at which time the accounts are closed. The service usually requires the debtor to surrender all of his or her credit cards in order to be eligible for assistance.

The credit counselor also reviews the debtor's financial picture to help the debtor set up a budget and plan expenses. There is usually no charge for the counseling, however, there may be a charge for managing the debt repayment plan. Some credit counseling agencies charge little or nothing for managing the plan while others charge a monthly fee that could add up to a significant charge over time. You should discuss this early in your meeting to make sure the services offered fit in your budget and will likely have a constructive outcome. Nevertheless, don't expect an overnight change in your situation as a successful repayment plan requires you to make regular, timely payments, and could take 48 months or longer to complete.

A debt repayment plan does not erase your credit history and creditors will continue to report information about accounts that are handled through a debt repayment plan. For example, creditors may report that an account is in financial counseling, that payments have been missed, or that there are write-offs or other concessions. But a demonstrated pattern of timely payments should help you obtain credit in the future.

## DEBT MANAGEMENT

### HOUSING COUNSELING AGENCIES

If you fall behind on your mortgage, contact your lender immediately to avoid foreclosure. Most lenders will work with you if they believe you're acting in good faith and the situation is temporary. Some lenders may reduce or suspend mortgage payments for a short time. Lenders may also agree to change the terms of the mortgage by extending the repayment period to reduce the monthly payments.

If you cannot work out a plan with your lender, you may consider contacting a housing counseling agency. Some agencies limit their counseling services to homeowners with FHA mortgages, but many offer free assistance to any homeowner having trouble making mortgage payments. If you have trouble locating a housing counseling agency, you can contact your local office of the Department of Housing and Urban Development (HUD), or the housing authority in your state, city, or county for a referral.

### DEBT CONSOLIDATION

Debt consolidation is the replacement of two or more loans with a single loan, usually with a lower monthly payment and a longer repayment period. To decide whether a debt consolidation proposal will work for you, add up your existing monthly minimum payments on all of your debts and compare them to what your payment will be if you consolidated all of those debts, including any fees. If you don't save at least 5 to 10% in monthly payments, it is not worth your while to consolidate.

#### Consolidating Student Loans

If you have more than one student loan from the federal government, you may be able to consolidate those loans and receive an interest rate reduction. This will lower your monthly payments and leave you with more money to pay off consumer debt.

#### Debt Consolidation Advertisements

The Federal Trade Commission (FTC) cautions consumers to read between the lines when faced with ads that advise the consumer to "consolidate their bills into one monthly payment without borrowing." Such advertisements often involve bankruptcy proceedings, which can seriously hurt your credit rating and cost an already debt-burdened consumer to incur attorneys' fees. Although bankruptcy is sometimes the only alternative available, it should be used as a last resort after all other means of paying one's debts have been investigated. Consumer bankruptcy is more fully discussed in Chapter 7 of this almanac.

# CHAPTER 3:
# TAX DEBTS

## INCOME TAXES

Federal and state taxing authorities are entitled to collect any income taxes you owe on your tax return but fail to pay. The first contact you get from the taxing authority will generally be a bill or notice of assessment telling you how much you owe. If they do not receive a payment or request for a payment plan, the next step is usually a final notice. Again, if there is no response, collection action may begin shortly thereafter. Taxing authorities are not required to file a legal action to obtain a judgment in order to collect taxes owed.

The debtor may be able to work out a payment plan for payment of their federal or state taxes, however, interest and penalties will continue to accrue. In order to have a payment plan approved, the debtor is generally required to complete a financial disclosure form. In the meantime, the taxing authority may stop collection action, but will likely file a lien against the debtor to protect their interests.

The federal tax collection procedures are discussed below. State tax collection procedures vary according to the state; therefore the reader is advised to check the law of his or her jurisdiction concerning state tax collection.

## INTERNAL REVENUE SERVICE TAX COLLECTION

### The Tax Bill

After a taxpayer's federal tax return is filed, the tax return is checked for mathematical accuracy, and the tax due is compared to all amounts paid. If there is any additional money owed, the taxpayer will be sent a bill. The issuance of the tax bill begins the tax collection process. The first bill sent explains the reason for the balance due and demands payment in full. It will include the tax due plus penalties and interest

# TAX DEBTS

that are added to the unpaid balance from the date the taxes were due. The calculation of interest and penalties are further discussed below.

The taxpayer should not ignore the bill but must either pay the tax due in full or make payment arrangements to satisfy their tax obligation, as discussed below. To ensure that the payment is properly credited to the taxpayer's account, the taxpayer should make their check or money order payable to the United States Treasury and notate the primary social security number or employer identification number, the tax year and form number, and their telephone number on their check or money order.

If the taxpayer believes the tax bill is inaccurate, they should contact the IRS office that sent the bill, by mail or telephone, or visit their nearest IRS office. The taxpayer should mail or bring a copy of the bill and copies of any records that support their position, such as the front and back of canceled checks or money orders, or other information that will help the IRS determine whether a mistake has been made. If you are communicating with the IRS by mail, it is important that you do not send original documents. You may also contact the IRS by telephone to discuss the bill. The IRS may be reached by calling 1-800-829-1040/ TTD: 1-800-829-4059.

If the bill is correct, but the taxpayer cannot pay the full amount due, they should pay as much as possible and immediately call the IRS to discuss payment of the remaining balance, as further discussed below.

### Interest and Penalties

The IRS charges interest, compounded daily, on any unpaid tax from the due date of the return until the date of payment. The interest rate is the federal short-term rate plus 3%. That rate is determined every three months. In addition, if the taxpayer files on time but doesn't pay on time, they will generally have to pay a late payment penalty of one-half of one percent of the tax owed for each month, or part of a month, that the tax remains unpaid after the due date, up to 25%. The one-half of one percent rate increases to one percent if the tax remains unpaid after several bills have been sent out and the IRS issues a notice of intent to levy.

If the taxpayer does not file on time and owes tax, they may owe an additional penalty for failure to file unless they can show reasonable cause. The combined penalty is 5 percent—a 4.5% late filing penalty and 0.5% late payment penalty—for each month, or part of a month, that the return was late, up to 25%. The late filing penalty applies to both the tax shown on the return and any additional tax found to be due, as reduced by any credits for withholding and estimated tax and any timely payments made with the return. After five months, if the taxpayer still has not paid the tax owed, the 0.5% failure-to-pay penalty continues to run, up to 25%, until the tax is paid. Thus, the total penalty for failure to file and pay can be 47.5%—a 22.5% late filing penalty and 25% late payment penalty—of the tax owed. Also, if the return was over 60 days late, the minimum failure-to-file penalty is the smallest of $100 or 100% of the tax required to be shown on the return.

The penalties for filing late and paying late may be waived if the taxpayer has reasonable cause for being late. If the taxpayer believes they have reasonable cause for being late, they should contact the IRS and provide them with their explanation. Generally, interest charges may not be waived; they continue to accrue until all assessed tax, penalties, and interest are paid in full.

### Installment Agreements

The taxpayer should file their return on time even if they cannot pay the entire amount owed. By filing on time, the late filing penalty is avoided. One should endeavor to pay as much of the amount owed as possible in order to reduce the amount of interest and late payment penalties assessed. If the taxpayer cannot pay the full amount due as shown on their tax return, they may ask to make monthly installment payments. However, they will be charged a one time user fee of $43.00, as well as interest on any tax not paid by its due date, and can be charged a late payment penalty unless they can show reasonable cause for not paying the tax by April 15, even if the request to pay in installments is granted. Before requesting an installment agreement, it is advisable to consider less costly alternatives such as a bank loan as the interest rate a bank charges may be lower than the combination of interest and penalties imposed by the Internal Revenue Code.

Even though the IRS may give the taxpayer an installment agreement, they may still file a Notice of Federal Tax Lien to secure the government's interest until the taxpayer makes the final payment. However, they cannot levy against the taxpayer's property during the following:

1. While the request for an installment agreement is being considered;

2. While the agreement is in effect;

3. For 30 days after the request for an agreement has been rejected; or

4. For any period while an appeal of the rejection is being evaluated by the IRS.

A sample IRS Installment Agreement Request Form is set forth at Appendix 3 of this almanac.

# TAX DEBTS

### Offer in Compromise

A taxpayer may qualify for an Offer in Compromise if they are unable to pay their taxes in full or if they are facing severe or unusual economic hardship. An Offer in Compromise is an agreement between a taxpayer and the Internal Revenue Service that resolves the taxpayer's tax liability. The ultimate goal is a resolution that is in both the government's and the taxpayer's best interest.

The IRS may legally compromise a tax liability for one of the following reasons:

1. Doubt as to Liability—There is doubt as to whether or not the assessed tax is correct;

2. Doubt as to Collectibility—There is doubt that the taxpayer could ever pay the full amount of the tax owed. However, the total amount owed must be greater than the sum of the taxpayer's assets and future income.

3. Promotion of Effective Tax Administration - There is no doubt that the assessed tax is correct and no doubt that the amount owed could be collected, but the taxpayer has an economic hardship or other special circumstances which may allow the IRS to accept less than the total balance due.

The IRS has the authority to settle, or compromise, federal tax liabilities by accepting less than full payment under certain circumstances, however, an Offer in Compromise is considered only after all other collection alternatives have been explored. The minimum offer amount must generally be equal to, or greater than, a taxpayer's reasonable collection potential (RCP). The RCP is defined as the total of the taxpayer's realizable value in real and personal assets, plus future income.

Thus, in determining an amount to offer in compromise of one's tax liability, the taxpayer should offer an amount that is equal to or exceeds the taxpayer's equity in assets, their ability to make installment payments from future income, amounts that can be collected from third parties on their behalf, and funds that are available to the taxpayer but not subject to IRS collection actions.

To apply for an Offer in Compromise, the taxpayer must file the appropriate application form and required attachments concerning their income, assets and debts, along with a $150 application fee, unless the offer is based solely on doubt as to liability. The fee may be waived if the taxpayer's total monthly income falls at or below income levels based on the Department of Health and Human Services poverty guidelines.

If the offer is accepted, the taxpayer may choose to pay the offer amount in a lump sum, in monthly payments over the remainder of the statutory time allowed for collection or a combination of a lump sum and monthly payments. Generally, it is to the taxpayer's advantage to pay the tax due in the shortest amount of time possible. Nevertheless, the IRS cannot consider an Offer in Compromise if the taxpayer is involved in an open bankruptcy proceeding or if they have not filed all federal tax returns.

**TAX COLLECTION PROCEDURES**

The IRS has considerable collection rights under the law that are not available to other debt collectors. For example, the IRS can share your tax information with city and state tax agencies, and can also contact third parties, such as neighbors, banks, and employers to investigate your case. If you ignore the tax bill and/or refuse to pay your tax or make payment arrangements, the IRS may take collection action, which could include:

1. Filing a Notice of Federal Tax Lien,

2. Serving a Notice of Levy; or

3. Offset of any refund due the taxpayer.

**Federal Tax Lien**

A federal tax lien gives the IRS legal claim to the taxpayer's property as security or payment for the outstanding tax liability. A federal tax lien attaches to all of the taxpayer's property, such as their house and car, and all their rights to property, such as their bank accounts. The law requires the IRS to notify the taxpayer, in writing, within 5 business days after the filing of a lien. Notice may be given in person, left at the taxpayer's home or usual place of business, or sent by certified or registered mail to the taxpayer's last known address. By filing a Notice of Federal Tax Lien, the Government provides public notice to creditors that the government has a claim against the taxpayer's property, including property that was acquired after the lien was filed. Once a lien is filed, it may harm the taxpayer's credit rating.

A Notice of Federal Tax Lien cannot be filed until:

1. The IRS assesses the taxpayer's liability;

2. The IRS sends the taxpayer a Notice and Demand for Payment—the bill that tells the taxpayer how much they owe in taxes; and

3. The taxpayer neglects or refuses to fully pay the debt within a certain number of days after the IRS notifies them about it.

### Release of Notice of Federal Tax Lien

When the tax is paid in full, along with any interest, penalties and lien recording fees, or becomes unenforceable, the IRS will issue a document known as a "Certificate of Release of Federal Tax Lien" which may be filed as evidence that the tax lien has been satisfied. The Release will generally be issued within 30 days after the taxpayer satisfies the tax liability. If the taxpayer submits a bond to the IRS that guarantees payment of the tax liability, the IRS will release the lien within 30 days after they accept the bond. In general, a tax lien is automatically released after the expiration of 10 years from the date the tax was assessed, if the IRS has not refiled the lien.

The Internal Revenue Service is required by law to timely release fully paid and unenforceable liens. If the taxpayer paid the tax, interest and penalties and did not receive a copy of the Certificate of Release of Federal Tax Lien, the taxpayer or authorized representative may call the Centralized Lien Processing Unit at the toll free number 1-800-913-6050.

If the IRS does not issue a Certificate of Release of Federal Tax Lien when it should be released, the taxpayer may sue the federal government for damages.

In addition, by law, a filed Notice of Federal Tax Lien may be withdrawn if:

1. The notice was filed too soon or not according to IRS procedures;

2. The taxpayer entered into an installment agreement to pay the debt on the notice of lien, unless the agreement provides otherwise;

3. Withdrawal will speed collecting the tax; or

4. Withdrawal would be in the taxpayer's best interest as determined by the Taxpayer Advocate, and in the best interest of the government.

### Filing an Appeal

The taxpayer may file an appeal within 30 days of the date they are given notice that the tax lien has been filed. Some valid bases for appeal include:

1. The taxpayer paid all the taxes owed before the IRS filed the lien;

2. The IRS assessed the tax and filed the lien when the taxpayer was in bankruptcy and subject to the automatic stay available during bankruptcy;

3. The IRS made a procedural error in an assessment;

4. The time to collect the tax—called the statute of limitations—expired before the IRS filed the lien,

5. The taxpayer did not have an opportunity to dispute the assessed liability,

6. The taxpayer wishes to discuss the collection options; or

7. The taxpayer wishes to make spousal defenses, e.g., an innocent spouse claim where the taxes were owed by one spouse but assessed against both because a joint return was filed.

At the conclusion of the appeal, the IRS Office of Appeals will issue a determination. That determination may support the continued existence of the filed federal tax lien or it may determine that the lien should be released or withdrawn. The taxpayer will have a 30-day period, starting with the date of the determination, to bring a suit to contest the determination in Tax Court.

### Federal Tax Levy

A levy is another method the IRS may use to collect taxes that are not paid voluntarily. A levy is a legal seizure of the taxpayer's property to satisfy a tax debt. A levy is not the same as a lien. A lien is a claim used as security for the tax debt whereas a levy actually takes the property to satisfy the tax debt. A levy means that the IRS, by legal authority, may take and sell the taxpayer's property to satisfy a tax debt. Levies can be made on property that the taxpayer holds, such as their car, boat, or house, or on property that belongs to the taxpayer but is held by a third party, such as wages held by an employer or funds on deposit at a bank.

### Levy Requirements

The IRS usually levies only after these three requirements are met:

1. The IRS assessed the tax and sent the taxpayer a Notice and Demand for Payment

2. The taxpayer neglected or refused to pay the tax; and

3. The IRS sent the taxpayer a Final Notice of Intent to Levy and a Notice of Right to Hearing at least 30 days before the levy.

As with a lien, notice may be given in person, left at the taxpayer's home or usual place of business, or sent to the taxpayer's last known address by certified mail, return receipt requested.

### Release of Levy

If the IRS levies the taxpayer's salary or wages, the levy will end when:

1. The levy is released;

2. The taxpayer pays the tax debt; or

3. The time expires for legally collecting the tax.

# TAX DEBTS

If the IRS levies the taxpayer's bank account, the bank is required to hold funds up to the amount of the tax liability for 21 days during which time the taxpayer may try and resolve any problems from the levy or make other payment arrangements. After the 21-day period expires, the bank must send the money being held, plus any applicable interest, to the IRS.

If the IRS makes a mistake in levying the taxpayer's bank account, the taxpayer may file a claim for reimbursement. In addition, if the taxpayer paid bank charges because of a mistake made, the taxpayer may be entitled to a reimbursement. To be reimbursed, the taxpayer must file a claim with the IRS within 1 year after their bank charged the fee.

The IRS must release the levy if any of the following occur:

1. The taxpayer pays the tax, penalty, and interest owed;

2. The IRS discovers that the time for collection ended before the levy was served;

3. The taxpayer provides documentation proving that releasing the levy will help the IRS collect the tax;

4. The taxpayer has, or is about to enter into, an approved, current installment agreement, unless the agreement says the levy does not have to be released;

5. The IRS determines that the levy is creating a significant economic hardship for the taxpayer.

6. The expense of selling the property would be more than the tax debt.

The IRS may release the taxpayer's levied property prior to the sale date if:

1. The taxpayer pays the amount of the government's interest in the property;

2. The taxpayer enters into an escrow arrangement;

3. The taxpayer furnishes an acceptable bond;

4. The taxpayer makes an acceptable agreement for paying the tax; or

5. The expense of selling the taxpayer's property would be more than the tax debt.

### Exemptions

By law, some property cannot be levied or seized including:

1. Schoolbooks and certain clothing;

2. Fuel, provisions, furniture, and personal effects for a household, totaling $7,200;

3. Books and tools used in the taxpayer's trade, business, or profession, totaling $3,600;

4. Unemployment benefits;

5. Undelivered mail;

6. Certain annuity and pension benefits;

7. Certain service-connected disability payments;

8. Worker's compensation benefits;

9. Salary, wages, or income included in a judgment for court-ordered child support payments;

10. Certain public assistance payments; or

11. A minimum weekly exemption for wages, salary, and other income.

The IRS may return levied property under certain circumstances, including:

1. If the IRS levies before they send the taxpayer two required notices;

2. If the IRS levies before the taxpayer's time for responding to the notices has passed—10 days for the Notice and Demand and 30 days for the Notice of Intent to Levy and the Notice of Right to Hearing.

3. If it was determined that the IRS did not follow their own procedures.

4. If the IRS agrees to let the taxpayer pay in installments;

5. Returning the property will help the taxpayer pay their taxes.

6. Returning the property is in both the taxpayer's best interest and the government's best interest.

### Tax Sale

After the taxpayer's property is seized, the IRS must usually wait 60 days before they can sell it. The IRS will post a public notice of a pending sale, usually in local newspapers or flyers and deliver the original notice of sale to the taxpayer or send it to the taxpayer by certified mail.

After placing the notice, the IRS must wait at least 10 days before conducting the sale, unless the property is perishable and must be sold immediately. Before the sale, the IRS will compute a minimum bid price.

# TAX DEBTS

This bid is usually 80% or more of the forced sale value of the property, after subtracting any liens. If the taxpayer disagrees with the minimum bid price, they can appeal it.

The taxpayer may also ask that the IRS sell the seized property within 60 days. The IRS will grant the taxpayer's request unless it is in the government's best interest to keep the property.

After the sale, the IRS first uses the proceeds to pay the expenses of the levy and sale. Then they use any remaining amount to pay the tax bill. If the proceeds of the sale are less than the total of the tax bill and the expenses of levy and sale, the taxpayer will still have to pay the unpaid tax.

If the proceeds of the sale are more than the total of the tax bill and the expenses of the levy and sale, the IRS will notify the taxpayer about the surplus money and will advise them on how to go about obtaining a refund. However, if someone, such as a mortgagee or other lienholder, makes a claim that is superior to that of the taxpayer, the IRS will pay that claim before they refund any money to the taxpayer.

### Redemption

The taxpayer or anyone with an interest in the taxpayer's property may redeem the property within 180 days after the sale by paying the purchaser the amount paid for the property, plus interest at 20% annually.

### Filing an Appeal

The taxpayer may file an appeal with the IRS Office of Appeals within 30 days of the date of the Final Notice of Intent to Levy and a Notice of Right to Hearing. Some valid bases for appeal include:

1. The taxpayer paid all taxes owed before the IRS sent the levy notice;

2. The IRS assessed the tax and sent the levy notice when the taxpayer was in bankruptcy and subject to the automatic stay available during bankruptcy;

3. The IRS made a procedural error in an assessment;

4. The time to collect the tax expired before the IRS sent the levy notice;

5. The taxpayer did not have an opportunity to dispute the assessed liability;

6. The taxpayer wishes to discuss the collection options; or

7. The taxpayer wishes to make spousal defenses, as set forth above.

As with a lien, at the conclusion of the appeal, the IRS Office of Appeals will issue a determination. That determination may support the levy action or it may determine that the levy should be released. The taxpayer will have a 30-day period, starting with the date of determination to bring a suit to contest the determination in Tax Court.

### IRS Taxpayer Advocate Program

The IRS offers special assistance on unresolved tax matters which are causing the taxpayer to suffer hardship. If the taxpayer is suffering, or is about to suffer a significant hardship because of the way Internal Revenue laws are being carried out against them, they may ask for special help from the IRS Taxpayer Advocate Program. However, before requesting this assistance the taxpayer should first attempt to use the existing administrative or formal appeal procedures. Most problems are resolved through regular channels. However, if any of the following circumstances apply, the taxpayer may ask for assistance from the Taxpayer Advocate Program:

1. The taxpayer is suffering or about to suffer a significant hardship.

2. The taxpayer is facing an immediate threat of adverse action.

3. The taxpayer will incur significant costs if relief is not granted, including fees for professional representation.

4. The taxpayer will suffer irreparable injury or long term adverse impact if relief is not granted.

5. The taxpayer has experienced a delay of more than 30 calendar days to resolve a tax-related problem or inquiry.

6. The taxpayer has not received a response or resolution to their problem by the date promised.

7. A system(s) or procedure(s) has either failed to operate as intended or failed to resolve the taxpayer's problem or dispute within the IRS.

If one or more of the above circumstances applies, the Taxpayer Advocate may issue a Taxpayer Assistance Order to suspend, delay, stop, or speed up IRS actions to relieve the taxpayer's hardship. Taxpayer Advocates cannot change the tax law or make a technical tax decision, however, they can clear up problems that resulted from previous contacts and ensure that the taxpayer's case is given a complete and impartial review. The IRS Taxpayer Advocate Program may be reached by calling 1-877-777-4778/TTD: 1-800-829-4059.

## PROPERTY TAXES

Homeowners are responsible for property taxes, which are generally made up of town taxes and school taxes. Property taxes are based on

## TAX DEBTS

the value of their property. Such taxes may include school taxes and municipal taxes, collectively referred to as property taxes. If you do not pay your property taxes within a prescribed period of time, a tax lien may be filed against your property to secure payment of the taxes.

A notice is given both to the property owner and mortgage holder, if any, when a property tax is delinquent. If the property owner does not have an escrow account in which funds are held to pay property taxes, the mortgage company may pay the tax and require the homeowner reimburse the company for the taxes paid.

If the tax lien is not paid within a certain amount of time after notices have been sent out, the property may be seized and sold at auction to the highest bidder. The minimum bid is generally the amount of back taxes owed plus interest and the costs of the sale. If the property is not sold, the government entity takes title and the property may be offered for sale to the public in a private transaction.

Depending on the state, following a tax deed sale, there may be a redemption period available to the debtor to regain his or her property by paying all taxes, interest and costs of the sale. Thus, individuals who purchase property at a tax deed sale are advised not to invest a lot of money into remodeling the property until the redemption period has lapsed.

# CHAPTER 4:
# THE DEBT COLLECTION PROCESS

## IN GENERAL

Debt collection is the process by which a creditor recovers money owed by individuals who are either unable or unwilling to pay their debts. When a due date passes with no recorded payment, the creditor's computer starts to churn out late notices, followed by telephone calls, and ultimately—if the amount is considerable—legal action to recover the debt. In the meantime, late fees and finance charges accrue, making it difficult for the debtor to catch up.

Many individuals become overwhelmed by this onslaught at a time when they are already vulnerable. Unethical creditors may prey on this vulnerability and try and recover debts by illegal means, such as using threatening language, misrepresenting the law, and using a variety of other pressure tactics. Thus, it is important that the debtor is aware of his or her rights and the laws designed to protect them should they find themselves in a financial bind.

If a consumer defaults on payments, the creditor will likely undertake some sort of debt collection. However, prior to being subjected to a formal lawsuit, one may wish to explore the possibility of an alternative method to resolve the dispute. If a debtor and creditor are unable to resolve the dispute in an informal manner, the creditor will likely attempt to recover the debt by suing the debtor in a court of law, particularly if the amount in dispute is significant.

A table of state statutes governing debt collection is set forth at Appendix 4 of this almanac.

## INTERNAL DEBT COLLECTION DEPARTMENTS

The first attempts to collect a debt are usually nonjudicial, and undertaken by the internal collection department of the creditor. Initial contacts are made by letter or telephone. Absent success, some debt

## THE DEBT COLLECTION PROCESS

collectors take increasingly invasive measures to collect the debt. If the creditor is unable to collect the debt voluntarily from the debtor, the creditor's remedy is usually limited to litigation to obtain a judgment against the debtor.

The first contact the debtor may receive from a creditor is usually a form letter—a polite reminder about the past due account. If the debtor doesn't respond with payment, however, the letters continue, with language that gets stronger with each mailing. One should not take these letters personally because they are computer-generated, and the computer can't distinguish one debtor from the next.

A sample Creditor Demand Letter is set forth in the Appendix 5 of this almanac.

The debtor may also receive several phone calls. If the debtor intends to pay the bill, but is unable to do so due to financial constraints, a payment plan can be requested. In the early stages of collection, most creditors are willing to work within the debtor's budget. Make sure that the proposed plan is realistic. It's not going to do much good to enter into a payment agreement and default on it.

The creditor will usually request the debtor to confirm the payment agreement in writing. Generally, a letter setting forth the agreement will be sent to the debtor, requesting that the debtor sign and return the letter. This gives the creditor an advantage if the debtor defaults on the agreement as it provides a written acknowledgement of the debt.

A sample Payment Agreement Confirmation Letter is set forth at Appendix 6 of this almanac.

A successful payment plan should start off slowly, proposing small payments for a number of months, with increases at various intervals. For example, a debtor who owes three hundred dollars on a revolving department store credit card may offer to pay twenty dollars per month for the first three months, increasing to fifty dollars per month for the next three months, etc. In this way, the creditor can see that there is some prospect of recovery in the near future.

The only problem with a payment plan is that the accrual of finance charges, late fees and/or over-the-limit fees often defeats the plan. After a significant number of payments are made, one may find that the principal is the same—if not higher—than when the payments began. Therefore, request that the creditor suspend these charges so all of your payments can be applied to reduce the principal. If so, the likelihood of success with the plan is increased. Some creditors will agree to waive these charges, others will absolutely refuse.

Companies usually establish a time period within which they try to collect a debt internally. If these efforts fail, and the creditor is unable to collect the debt or make a satisfactory payment agreement with the debtor, the creditor will generally place the account with an attorney or independent collection agency with whom the creditor contracts.

**INDEPENDENT DEBT COLLECTION AGENCIES**

Independent debt collection agencies generally earn a percentage of any amount they are able to collect. Thus, their business depends on getting money from you. Intimidation is central to their success. They are notorious for using threats, humiliation, misrepresentation, and other forms of harassment to get you to pay. It is important that you remain calm in response to these contacts and know your rights under the law.

As further discussed in this almanac, there are laws governing debt collection agency conduct with which they must comply or face legal consequences. For example, a debtor has the right to advise the collection agency that he or she no longer wishes any telephone contact concerning the debt. This notice should be in writing, and sent to the collection agency by certified mail with a return receipt requested. If the collection agency continues to make telephone contact concerning the debt, this is a violation, and the debt collector may be held liable for damages.

A sample Notice to Collection Agency to Cease Contact is attached at Appendix 7 of this almanac.

Do not give the collector what he or she wants, which is to scare you into handing over some money. Realize that there is little that they can do, despite the many threats one may read and hear. For example, one common tactic is to continually telephone the debtor. The purpose of these telephone calls is not only to demand payment, but also to try and persuade the debtor to converse and give information that may be helpful in the collection of the debt or enforcement of a judgment.

Some debt collectors request that the debtor provide them with post-dated checks even though the debtor states that their account does not presently have sufficient funds. The debt collector may assure the debtor that the check will not be processed without his or her consent. Don't fall for this routine. The debt collector often employs this tactic so that, if the check is dishonored, he or she can threaten the debtor with criminal bad check prosecution.

Although prosecution for bad checks is unlikely in this scenario, the mere threat can still be unsettling. It is wise not to place oneself in this position in the first instance. In any event, under certain circumstances, using this tactic may expose the debt collector to liability for damages sustained by the debtor.

The reader is advised to check the law of his or her own jurisdiction concerning the application and limitations of criminal bad check statutes.

The debt collector may also threaten immediate legal action to collect the debt. This is unlikely, particularly when they are dealing with a relatively small amount. The costs of litigation are high and often exceed the debt. Using a cost-benefit analysis, it is simply bad business to litigate every bad debt. When the amount is relatively small, most creditors will at some point simply take the loss—also known as a "charge off"—and satisfy themselves with ruining your credit rating.

Further, it is a violation for a debt collector to threaten legal action which is not intended to be taken. Also note that it is illegal for a collection agency to send you a form that appears to be a court document, such as a document resembling an official summons.

Another common tactic some collectors use is to tell the debtor that they are going to "take their home" or "garnishee their wages" if the debt is not paid within a certain amount of time. Despite what you are told by the collector—unless it pertains to taxes—the debt collector cannot immediately "take your home" or actually "collect" any money by attaching your assets or wages, unless they first obtain a judgment. Note, however, that the requirement of obtaining a judgment does not apply to the taxing authorities, such as the Internal Revenue Service.

When you are subjected to abusive collection tactics, simply inform the collector that they are misrepresenting themselves, and that you know your rights. You can even spell it out for them in detail by reciting the applicable law. Debt collectors dislike communicating with debtors who know their rights and can't be coerced. Ask the debt collector if you can tape the conversation for your records. This will likely intimidate the debt collector, and you may find that he or she actually hangs up the phone on you for a change.

The oppressive and abusive measures that debt collection agencies have been known to take has led to federal and state legislation designed to protect debtors. In addition, there exist a number of common law theories under which an aggrieved debtor can retaliate against unfair debt collection procedures. Thus, it is important to be aware of your rights. If a collector violates your legal rights, you can sue and recover money for your damages. You may even be able to get the debt canceled. Your right to pursue legal action for debt collection harassment is further discussed in Chapter 5.

If you are faced with a particularly offensive collection agency, you may also want to notify the original creditor. Most times, the original creditor is unaware of the tactics used by the collection agency with which it contracts. Advise the original creditor that you plan to take legal action, and send a copy of the letter to the appropriate governmental agencies, as well as your attorney. You may gain some satisfaction in knowing that an abusive collection agency loses a client.

## NONJUDICIAL DEBT COLLECTION

As discussed below, there are a number of methods by which a debtor can try and resolve a debt with the creditor before the creditor seeks to recover the debt by filing a formal legal action.

### Compromise and Settlement

If you are concerned about protecting your credit rating, or want to avoid a lawsuit, you may consider compromising and settling the debt. The debt collector has an incentive to settle the matter, so that they can move on to other accounts, and receive their commission on your debt.

Creditors will usually consider accepting a reduced amount provided that the reduced amount is paid in full. If you have access to a lump sum of money, it may be worthwhile to offer the creditor an amount far below what is actually owed. For example, you may be able to reduce a three thousand dollar debt to fifteen hundred dollars—a fifty percent reduction—if you are able to come up with the lump sum of money by the agreed upon date.

As further discussed in Chapter 8, there are agencies who advertise their ability to intervene on behalf of the debtor and work out agreements for repayment of the debt. However, if you are considering using such a service, it is crucial to fully investigate the background and reputation of such a company.

Even if the lawsuit has been filed, the parties can still settle the matter by entering into a stipulation. However, if the debtor defaults, the stipulation may provide that a judgment can be entered immediately upon default.

A sample Agreement to Compromise a Debt is set forth at Appendix 8 of this almanac.

### Arbitration and Mediation

Another method of resolving a dispute without formal legal action is through arbitration or mediation. Many contracts provide for arbitration or mediation as the agreed methods to resolve a dispute. If there is no such prior agreement, the parties can also stipulate to arbitrate or mediate the dispute. The process is usually more economical and expedient than a trial. In an arbitration, the decision of the arbiter is binding on the parties. In a mediation, the mediator tries to assist the parties in reaching a mutually satisfying resolution, however, if the mediation is unsuccessful, the creditor is free to resort to more formal methods of debt recovery.

A more detailed discussion of arbitration and mediation may be found in this author's legal almanac entitled *The Law of Dispute Resolution*, also published by Oceana Publishing Company.

### Confession of Judgment

A debt collector may ask the debtor to sign a confession of judgment in return for the cessation of all collection activities. A confession of judgment is an affidavit executed by the debtor that basically admits that the debtor owes the debt, and authorizes entry of a judgment in a certain sum. A confession of judgment gives the creditor the right to collect on the debt without requiring them to file a legal action to obtain a judgment. Signing a confession of judgment is not advisable, particularly if the debtor is looking to buy some time to satisfy the debt.

## JUDICIAL DEBT COLLECTION

Most creditors will not pursue legal action to recover a relatively small debt, particularly if the projected costs of the action outweigh the recovery. However, if the debt is substantial enough to warrant a lawsuit, the creditor may seek to obtain a judgment to recover the debt.

### Statute of Limitations

In order to take legal action to recover a debt, the legal action must be commenced within the applicable statute of limitations. A statute of limitations refers to the period within which an action must be commenced by law. Different types of actions carry different time periods. For example, some jurisdictions provide that a contract action must be commenced within six years, whereas a personal injury lawsuit must be commenced within three years. The reader is advised to check the laws of his or her jurisdiction concerning the applicable statute of limitations.

### The Litigation Process

Litigation to recover a debt begins with the filing of a lawsuit with the court. This is accomplished by service of a summons and complaint upon the debtor. Service is undertaken by a person authorized by law to serve legal documents, such as the sheriff or a process server. Many jurisdictions also permit a non-party, over the age of 18, to serve legal documents.

Depending on the jurisdiction, the party bringing the lawsuit is known as the plaintiff or petitioner, and the party against whom the lawsuit is filed is known as the defendant or respondent. The complaint details the plaintiff's claim against the defendant, and sets forth the legal theory under which the plaintiff seeks to prevail.

Upon receipt of the summons and complaint, the defendant must respond to the complaint within a prescribed period of time or risk losing the dispute by default. The defendant may serve an answer to the complaint, or may choose to make a motion seeking to dismiss the complaint prior to serving his or her answer. If the motion is granted, the case is dismissed. However, if the motion is denied, the defendant must serve an answer within a statutorily defined time period following the decision on the motion.

The defendant's answer admits or denies the allegations set forth in the complaint, and presents any defenses to the allegations that the defendant may have. Additionally, if the defendant has his or her own claims against the plaintiff, known as counterclaims, these allegations are also set forth in the defendant's answer. The plaintiff is then required to serve an answer addressing the counterclaim.

The litigation procedure, from initiation of the lawsuit to final disposition, is governed by the statutory law of the particular court in which the lawsuit is filed. During the pendency of the lawsuit, much of litigation is accomplished on paper. There are numerous motions that a party may file and ask the assigned judge to rule upon. A motion, which may be made orally or in writing, is an application to the court requesting an order or a ruling in favor of the applicant.

For example, a party may make a motion seeking some type of interim relief, such as the production of certain evidence. This may include, for example, proof that a debt is owed. The notice of motion and any supporting papers are served upon the other party, who usually responds in opposition to the motion.

Complex litigation usually involves a lengthy discovery process. Typical discovery may include the exchange of detailed information, the examination of documents and other evidence, and an oral examination of the parties and prospective witnesses in a proceeding known as a deposition or examination before trial.

During a deposition, the deponent is placed under oath, and must answer a series of questions asked by the parties or their attorneys. The sworn testimony given at the deposition is recorded by a legal stenographer, who prepares a transcript of the depositions for use at trial. The deposition testimony pins down each deponent's version of the facts, and can be used to impeach a party or non-party witness.

## THE DEBT COLLECTION PROCESS

As the lawsuit nears trial, the judge will usually set the matter down for a settlement conference, in an attempt to resolve the dispute without going to trial. Absent a successful outcome, the lawsuit eventually goes to trial, after which a decision is rendered by the judge or jury. The parties may seek to appeal unfavorable decisions to higher courts. Once the appeals process has been exhausted, the decision is final and a prevailing plaintiff will be awarded an enforceable judgment.

As the above demonstrates, protracted litigation over a debt is in nobody's best interest. Legal fees for both the plaintiff and defendant could prove costly. It is unlikely that the defendant, who is already in debt, would be able to afford an attorney to handle the litigation. However, individuals have the right to represent themselves in a lawsuit. This is known as acting "pro se," and can be a creditor's nightmare. At this point, the creditor may be willing to take a reasonable offer below the debt amount. However, if you believe that you do not owe the debt, then by all means, you should try and fight it.

As set forth above, if you decide not to answer the complaint within the time required, you will be considered "in default." A default judgment will thereafter be awarded the plaintiff. Of course, this means that collection can begin in a relatively short period of time following commencement of the action. Thus, the debtor is advised to act immediately upon receipt of a summons and complaint. Judgment enforcement is discussed more fully in Chapter 6 of this almanac.

# CHAPTER 5:
# DEBT COLLECTION HARASSMENT

### IN GENERAL

In most instances, people do not intentionally fail to pay their valid debts. Studies have shown that the primary reasons people fall into debt are loss of employment, health reasons, or a change in family status, such as divorce. These scenarios are certain to be a source of great stress to an individual who previously was able to responsibly manage his or her finances.

Thus, the debtor is quite vulnerable to the often abusive tactics used by debt collectors. The consequences can be devastating. The emotional stress can lead to serious physical conditions, such as ulcers and heart attacks. A debt collector who continually telephones a debtor at his or her place of employment can jeopardize the debtor's job.

Recognizing the serious nature of this problem, federal and state laws have been enacted to protect the debtor from illegal collection tactics. The debtor is entitled to take legal action against the offending debt collector. Different statutes afford the debtor different types of relief.

The prohibited practices and available remedies under the federal Fair Debt Collection Practices Act are set forth below. In addition, state statutes may provide the debtor with additional relief. Depending on the violation, the debtor may be able to pursue remedies under both federal and state law. The reader is advised to consult the law of his or her own jurisdiction to determine the relief available under state law.

### ALTERNATIVES TO LITIGATION

If the debtor wishes to put an end to debt collection harassment but does not necessarily want to sue, there are a number of alternatives which may be explored. For example, the debtor can request, in writing, that they receive no further telephone contact concerning the debt.

Once such a written request is received, a collection agency must comply.

The letter should be sent to the collection agency by certified mail with a return receipt requested. This will give the debtor written proof of the date the collection agency received the letter. Copies of the letter should be sent to the original creditor, and to the appropriate state and federal agencies. If the debtor's request is not honored, the next letter should come from an attorney, with a warning that legal action will be taken if the contact continues.

A sample Notice to Collection Agency to Cease Contact is set forth at Appendix 7.

## GATHERING EVIDENCE

Sometimes the debt collector's behavior is so egregious, and such a blatant violation of the debt collection laws, that it should be challenged. Of course, one needs proof to pursue a lawsuit, otherwise it would be the debtor's word against the collector. Thus, it is important for the debtor to keep accurate notes of every telephone call received from the debt collector. The notes should include the times and dates of the telephone calls, the name and telephone number of the person making the contact, and the actual language used by the collector, including quotes of any particularly threatening or abusive statements.

Depending on the law of the jurisdiction, it may be legal to tape the conversations you have with debt collectors, without telling them that they are being taped. Most answering machines now have the capability of taping a telephone conversation. If there are debt collectors telephoning you who are violating the law—e.g., using profane and threatening language—a tape recording will certainly bolster your case if you decide to take legal action against them.

Of course, it is essential for the reader to check the laws of his or her jurisdiction on the legality of taping without consent, so as to avoid violating any statutes. It is generally considered unethical for an attorney to tape a telephone conversation without the knowledge of all parties.

If the law prevents taping the telephone conversation, an alternative would be to have a third party—as a potential witness—listen to the conversation on an extension or by way of three-way calling. The witness should take detailed notes concerning the conversation.

In addition, if you continue to receive collection letters dated after the return receipt date of your notice to cease contact, this may indicate a violation has taken place. Save all of the correspondence you receive from the debt collection agency for review by your attorney.

## COMMON LAW THEORIES OF RECOVERY

In addition to the remedies available under federal and state law, the debtor can seek further relief under a number of common law legal theories. Common law refers to decisions rendered by judges in civil cases as opposed to statutory law. Thus, a common law tort action may give the debtor broader recovery because the debtor's relief is not confined to that provided for in the statute.

For example, depending on the jurisdiction, if the debtor is able to prove malicious, willful or reckless conduct, punitive damages may be available under common law even if the statute does not provide for such damages.

In addition, in a common law tort action, the debtor may be able to sue parties who would not otherwise be amenable to suit under the applicable statutes. For example, the *Fair Debt Collection Practices Act* only covers the debt collection agency, and not the original creditor.

The reader is advised to check the laws of his or her jurisdiction for the specific elements which need to be proven to make out a prima facie case for each potential common law actions.

Two common law theories that are most applicable to debt collection harassment include intentional infliction of emotional distress; and intentional interference with business relationships.

### Intentional Infliction of Emotional Distress

Intentional infliction of emotional distress is a claim of tortious—wrongful—conduct on the part of the tortfeasor—the wrongdoer—that intentionally or recklessly causes mental distress to the victim. The defendant's conduct must generally be outrageous or unreasonable, however, exactly what constitutes outrageous or unreasonable conduct is a question to be decided by the trier of fact. Guidelines may be found in the federal and state statutes and case law. A minority of jurisdictions may require that the emotional distress manifest itself in some type of physical injury.

An example of an intentional infliction of emotional distress claim is an allegation that a creditor repeatedly telephoned the debtor's home and, in speaking with the debtor and family members, used profane and threatening language, which caused the debtor and his family to suffer severe mental distress and humiliation.

### Intentional Interference with Business Relationships

A common tactic used by debt collectors is to put pressure on the debtor to pay by involving his or her employer. For example, a debt collector may telephone the employer directly, or knowing that the debtor is not allowed personal calls at work, may place the debtor's job in jeopardy by repeatedly calling the debtor at his or her place of business. If the debtor can demonstrate that loss of employment was caused by the debt collector's actions, he or she may prevail on this theory.

### Miscellaneous Common Law Theories of Recovery

Depending on the specific factual allegations, other applicable common law theories of recovery may include defamation, invasion of privacy, malicious prosecution, assault and battery, extortion, and fraud. In addition, a debt collector's actions may violate state criminal laws, and statutes prohibiting the unauthorized practice of law.

## ASSESSING DAMAGES

Damages commonly alleged in debt collection harassment cases include actual out-of-pocket costs, and emotional injuries with any attendant physical illness. Out-of-pocket costs may include such items as attorney fees, lost wages, and medical expenses. Most debt collection statutes include some type of statutory damages above out-of-pocket expenses.

Depending on the statute, a debtor may also be entitled to recover for the pain and suffering caused by the misconduct. Placing a dollar amount on such damages is difficult. The trier-of-fact must depend on evidence in making an award. For example, if the debtor has suffered mental distress as a result of threatening and abusive collection tactics, in addition to the debtor's own testimony, there should be testimony from a medical professional as to the existence and extent of the injury.

In addition, a debt collector's conduct may be so malicious or reckless as to warrant the assessment of punitive damages. The purpose of punitive damages is to punish the offender, and to deter similar behavior and future violations by the offender and other debt collection agencies.

## CAUSATION

To prevail in a debt collection harassment case, the debtor must be able to demonstrate that his or her injuries were caused by the debt collector's illegal acts. This can present problems. For example, it can be presumed that an individual who has fallen into debt is already under stress. The debtor must be able to show how the illegal collection tactics added to the debtor's suffering.

In addition, the debtor may have been contacted by a number of debt collectors, some or most of whom operated within the bounds of the law. The debtor must be able to connect his or her injuries to the misconduct of the offending collectors, and the degree to which each is responsible must be analyzed.

## THE FAIR DEBT COLLECTION PRACTICES ACT

### In General

Many of the state debt collection harassment statutes are patterned after the *Fair Debt Collection Practices Act* (FDCPA). In addition, the debtor may find remedies in the *Federal Trade Commission Act*. Section 5 of the Act governs unfair or deceptive acts or practices in connection with debt collection. The Federal Trade Commission (FTC) will investigate activities that can lead to law enforcement action

A copy of the FTC Online Consumer Complaint Form is set forth at Appendix 9 of this almanac.

In 1988, the *Fair Debt Collection Practices Act* was enacted to supplement the available statutory and common law tort remedies available to the debtor to restrain unfair debt collection procedures. The Act contains detailed provisions regulating the manner in which debt collection is carried out. However, the Act applies only to debt collection agencies whereas the state statutes modeled after the Act generally apply to creditors as well. Attorneys are not included in the definition of debt collector under the Act.

Personal, family, and household debts are covered under the Act, including money owed for the purchase of an automobile, for medical care, or for charge accounts.

### Obligations of Debt Collectors

The *Fair Debt Collection Practices Act* requires debt collectors to provide information about the alleged debt, and verification of the debt, at the request of the consumer, including the name of the creditor, the amount of the debt, and an offer to provide the name of the original creditor, if different.

In addition, a statement must be sent, generally with the first communication, advising the debtor that the debt will be assumed valid if he or she fails to dispute its validity within 30 days. If the debtor disputes the validity of the date, the debt collector must verify the debt with the credit grantor.

A sample letter to a credit card issuer disputing an item reported by the credit grantor is set forth at Appendix 10 of this almanac.

**Prohibited Practices**

The *Fair Debt Collection Practices Act* prohibits various kinds of collection practices, including, but not limited to:

1. Communicating with the debtor at an unusual or inconvenient time or place;

2. Communicating with the debtor at his or her place of employment if the employer prohibits such communications, or if the debtor requests that he or she not be contacted there;

3. Communicating with a debtor who is represented by an attorney;

4. Communicating with third parties without the authorization of the debtor;

5. Communicating with the debtor after he or she has notified the debt collector to cease communication concerning the debt. In this case, the debt collector may not contact the debtor except for the limited purpose of advising the debtor, in writing, of further action to be taken;

6. Making false, deceptive or misleading representations;

7. Using unfair or unconscionable conduct to collect the debt; and

8. Using harassing, threatening or otherwise abusive conduct to collect the debt.

If the debtor has an attorney, the debt collector must contact the attorney, rather than the debtor. If the debtor does not have an attorney, a collector may contact other people, but only to find out the debtor's address, telephone number, and place of employment. Debt collectors are usually prohibited from contacting such third parties more than once. In most cases, the collector may not tell anyone other than the debtor and their attorney that the debtor owes money.

In addition, a debt collector may not contact the debtor if, within 30 days after the debtor receives written notice of the debt, they send the collection agency a letter stating they do not owe the money. However, a collector can renew collection activities if they send you proof of the debt, such as a copy of a bill for the amount owed. A debt collector may not apply a payment to any debt the debtor believes they do not owe. If the debtor owes more than one debt, any payment they make must be applied to the debt they indicate as valid.

### Remedies

If a debt collector violates any of the provisions of the *Fair Debt Collection Practices Act*, he or she is liable to the person with whom the violation took place. This would include the debtor and any other persons who were subject to the debt collector's improper tactics. The statute of limitations on bringing an action under the Act is one year.

The debtor is entitled to actual damages, including physical or emotional injury, and actual expenses. The debtor is also entitled to statutory damages of up to One Thousand ($1,000.00) Dollars as set forth in the Act, whether or not actual damages exist, and whether or not the violation was intentional or inadvertent. Debtors who prevail on their claim may also be entitled to legal fees and costs at the discretion of the court.

The text of the *Fair Debt Collection Practices Act* is set forth at Appendix 11 and a sample Complaint brought under the FDCPA for debt collection harassment is set forth at Appendix 12 of this almanac.

# CHAPTER 6:
# JUDGMENT ENFORCEMENT

**IN GENERAL**

If a creditor prevails in a legal action against the debtor for the amount owed, the court awards the creditor a "judgment" for money damages. The creditor is thereafter known as a judgment creditor and the defendant as the judgment debtor. If the judgment debtor does not voluntarily pay on the judgment amount, the plaintiff may attempt to "execute" on the judgment—i.e., recover the amount owed.

Collecting a debt from an individual or business that is solvent is not as difficult because the judgment debtor purportedly has some interests to protect, e.g., a good credit rating. However, when the debtor is insolvent, or appears to be "judgment proof"—i.e., has no discernable assets from which to collect the debt—or is simply reluctant to pay the debt, further debt collection techniques must be employed to recover the money owed the creditor.

**THE JUDGMENT PROOF DEBTOR**

As set forth above, a debtor who has no assets or wages that can be attached or garnished is often referred to as "judgment proof." For example, a senior citizen, who rents his or her living space, and survives on social security, without any assets except for those that would be deemed exempt, would be considered "judgment proof." An unemployed college student, with no discernable assets, would also likely be considered "judgment proof."

However, if it appears that the debtor's financial situation will change in the future—e.g., the college student will embark on a promising new career after graduation—depending on the jurisdiction, a judgment creditor may patiently await the change in financial circumstances because they generally have a long time to enforce a judgment and collect the debt, e.g. ten or more years. Once the statutorily prescribed time period ends, however, the debt is presumed satisfied unless the judgment debtor acknowledges the debt or makes a payment during that period. Depending on the jurisdiction, either of these actions could renew and/or extend the time period for collection.

## FINANCIAL DISCLOSURE

In order to determine whether the judgment debtor is solvent, the judgment creditor is entitled to inquire into the debtor's assets, and the debtor must comply. This information is obtained in a number of ways, depending on the jurisdiction and the court in which the judgment was awarded.

For example, the debtor or a third party, such as a bank, may be served with a subpoena requiring the debtor or other appropriate person to answer, under oath, a number of questions concerning the location and amount of the judgment debtor's assets. The subpoena may also call for the production of financial records. Failure to comply with the subpoena may result in a contempt proceeding and lead to court-ordered punishment for the offending party.

If the judgment creditor is able to uncover assets belonging to the judgment debtor, the judgment creditor may serve a restraining notice on the judgment debtor or a third party who is in possession of judgment debtor's assets, such as a bank.

## RESTRAINING NOTICE

A restraining notice instructs the judgment debtor, or a third party, that he or she cannot transfer or dispose of any assets of the judgment debtor. The restraining notice is not a levy or a lien on the assets, as further discussed below. It merely prevents their transfer until the judgment creditor acquires a levy or lien on the assets at which time the sheriff or other authorized law enforcement officer seizes the property.

Nevertheless, if the property which is the subject of the execution is "exempt," as further discussed below, the debtor can make a claim for exemption and the officer would be prevented from seizing the exempt property.

## METHODS OF JUDGMENT ENFORCEMENT

### In General

Whether a judgment is awarded as a result of a litigated dispute, a confession of judgment, or a default, the collection procedures are the same. There are a number of methods by which a creditor may enforce a judgment and recover a debt from a debtor. For example, the creditor may seize money from a debtor's bank account, attach the debtor's business income or garnish a portion of a debtor's wages. The creditor may also be able to seize personal or real property owned by the debtor, or money owed to the debtor by third parties.

If a creditor creates a lien on the real property of the debtor, the creditor will generally get paid when the property is sold or refinanced. The lien may arise by agreement, statute, or through litigation between the parties. The proceeds from the sale of the debtor's property are used to satisfy the debt to the creditor.

In some states, a lien is automatically created when the court enters its judgment. In others, you must file a document to create a lien. Although recovering a debt by filing a lien on the property may take a long time, it requires little effort on the part of the creditor, who merely waits for the sale or refinance to occur. In addition, every state authorizes a creditor to collect interest on a debt—generally at a statutory rate—while waiting to get paid.

### Attachment and Garnishment

Attachment and garnishment are the two most common remedies available to a judgment creditor to recover money owed by the judgment debtor. Attachment is a limited statutory remedy whereby a creditor has the property of a debtor seized to satisfy the debt. The process of "attachment and execution" permits a creditor, with the assistance of the sheriff or marshal, to take or "seize" the debtor's personal property—such as a car—and then sell it. Thus, attachment refers to taking legal possession of the debtor's property and execution refers to the sale of the attached property to satisfy the debt.

Garnishment refers to the process of taking something belonging to the debtor which is being held by a third party, known as the "garnishee." For example, if a creditor "garnishes" a debtor's bank account, the bank is the "garnishee" because the bank is holding the funds in the debtor's account.

The remedies of attachment and garnishment are similar in many respects. Both are statutory remedies, and Federal courts follow state rules as to the availability of one or both remedies. In many states, the terms attachment and garnishment are used interchangeably and, in fact, garnishment is often referred to as a form of attachment. In some states, garnishment is not a separate remedy but rather a proceeding ancillary to attachment, while in other states, garnishment is an independent remedy.

The primary difference between attachment and garnishment is that attachment is directed to property in the possession of the debtor, whereas garnishment is directed to the property of the debtor that is being held by the garnishee. Attached property is seized pending execution whereas garnished property is generally left in the care and custody of the garnishee until surrendered to the creditor.

Thus, through attachment and garnishment, a creditor collects, applies or subjects personal property, real property, wages or funds, owned by or due to a debtor, to the debt owed to the creditor. Any claim, which is due from one person to another whether arising from a personal loan, installment purchase, tort action, contract action or any other action can be satisfied in whole or part by the use of attachment or garnishment proceedings.

### Wage Garnishment

A judgment creditor may "garnish" a judgment debtor's wages to satisfy a debt. Depending on the jurisdiction, the creditor is entitled to a statutorily prescribed percentage of the debtor's net pay. Generally, the sheriff will serve the employer with a wage garnishment. The employer must then deduct the statutory amount from the debtor's paycheck and forward it to the sheriff. The sheriff office deducts its fee, and the balance is sent to the judgment creditor.

The federal government has limited wage garnishment so that no amount may be withheld for any week unless the debtor's disposable earnings exceed thirty times the federal minimum hourly wage as prescribed in the Fair Labor Standard Act in effect at the time the earnings are payable.

### Bank Execution

The judgment creditor may make an application to the court for an execution on the bank account of the judgment debtor. The bank execution gives the creditor permission to allow the sheriff to seize the proceeds of the debtor's bank account.

After the bank execution is issued, the sheriff serves the execution on the debtor's bank. The bank must notify the debtor of the execution. After a prescribed period of time—e.g., 15 days—if the debtor does not claim an exemption, the bank must turn the funds over to the sheriff. The sheriff office deducts its fee, and the balance is sent to the judgment creditor.

The debtor has the right to petition the court if he or she believes that the money in the bank account is exempt, e.g., the funds are social security or unemployment compensation income.

### Property Execution

A property execution is usually delivered to the sheriff, or other designated enforcement officer, so that he or she can enforce it. The sheriff will then demand payment and place a levy on the judgment debtor's assets. The judgment creditor must specify the type, amount and whereabouts of the debtor's assets in the execution.

The sheriff is obligated to levy the property specifically identified by the creditor so as to avoid dissipation of the assets. The manner in which a levy takes place generally involves delivery of the property execution to the custodian of the property, inspection and inventory of the property, and may also involve the physical relocation of the property. Property subject to execution may be sold at a public auction.

### Real Property Execution

A judgment creditor may file a lien against the judgment debtor's home or other real property. However, unless the amount of the debt is significant, it is not likely that the creditor would proceed with a foreclosure and sale of the home to recover the debt, as this is a costly undertaking. Nevertheless, the mere filing of a lien against one's home is often enough to get a debtor to negotiate a settlement. In any event, the debtor is prevented from refinancing or selling the home until the lien is satisfied.

### Homestead Exemption

Some states provide the debtor with a certain level of protection under a law generally known as a "homestead exemption." Depending on the jurisdiction, this may completely protect the debtor's home from a foreclosure sale or, at the very least, may provide the debtor with the exemption amount if the home is sold to satisfy the debt. Nevertheless, if the collector is a taxing authority, a homestead exemption may not be available. Further, if the debtor defaults on his or her mortgage, the lender can foreclose on the property and force a sale.

Depending on the jurisdiction, the law may provide a redemption period following a forced sale of the debtor's home. During this period of time, the debtor may be able to regain ownership to the property by paying off the debt, as well as court costs and other expenses. The reader is advised to check the applicable redemption laws of his or her jurisdiction.

### Construction Lien

A construction lien—also referred to as a mechanic's lien—is a claim created by law which allows for a lien to be placed against real property for labor performed or materials furnished that contributed to an improvement made on that property. The lien remains in effect until the person performing the labor or furnishing the materials has been paid in full. In the event the property is sold or otherwise disposed of, the lien holder is given priority of payment ahead of other creditors.

### Statutory Exemptions

In order to afford some degree of protection to the judgment debtor, each state has designated certain items that are exempt from execution, such as the homestead exemption discussed above. Depending on the law, other exempt items may include an automobile, retirement pension, social security income, clothing and personal items. The reader is advised to check the law of his or her own jurisdiction to determine the applicable exemptions, and the procedure to follow to claim the exemption.

### Satisfaction of Judgment and Release of Lien

When a judgment is paid, a satisfaction of judgment and release of lien, if applicable, must be filed with the proper authorities within a certain time period after the payment is made. A copy of the satisfaction of judgment is usually required to be sent to the judgment debtor. If the judgment is paid, in part, a partial satisfaction of judgment may be filed.

A sample satisfaction of judgment and release of lien is set forth at Appendix 13.

## WRONGFUL ATTACHMENT OR GARNISHMENT

Although many precautions are taken by the courts in issuing attachment or garnishment orders, there are times when the order is improperly or fraudulently obtained. In these cases, the debtor has some options to pursue to obtain compensation for his or her damages, as set forth below.

### Malicious Prosecution Action

A malicious prosecution action requires the debtor to show that he or she was the successful party in an action which determined the validity of the attachment. Further, the debtor must usually show that the creditor brought the attachment proceeding maliciously, without probable cause. The debtor must further show that he or she was damaged in some respect. Most states require a wrongful sequestration of the debtor's property before the court will entertain a malicious prosecution suit.

Even if the creditor eventually wins in the primary suit against the debtor, the attachment may still be wrongful if adequate grounds did not exist. Each state has its own requirements for malicious prosecution suits. Some states require a showing of malice on the part of the creditor while other states require a showing of a lack of probable cause.

### Liability on the Attachment or Garnishment Bond

Another remedy for wrongful attachment is for the debtor to sue on the attachment or garnishment bond, if one was required. Most states generally require that before an attachment or garnishment shall issue, the creditor must post a bond conditioned to pay the costs and damages that the debtor may sustain if the order was wrongfully issued. The right to bring an action on such a bond depends upon the obligations specifically set forth in the bond.

### Abuse of Process Actions

The abuse of process action is generally brought where there has been an excessive garnishment or attachment—i.e., where the creditor has attached more of the debtor's property or obtained a greater garnishment against him than was necessary to secure the debt owed.

### Damages

The statutes of each state determine the type and extent of damages recoverable in an action for wrongful attachment or garnishment. Normally, the defendant can recover all the actual damages that he sustained as a natural result of the wrongful attachment or garnishment. Unusual, remote or speculative damages are generally not recoverable.

#### Compensatory Damages

Compensatory damages are those damages which attempt to place the debtor back in the position he or she was in prior to the wrongful act. If property has been lost or destroyed, the debtor may recover the value of the property at the time it was seized. If the goods were damaged, the debtor may recover the value prior to the damage. Damages caused by a detention of the property may be recoverable as well as the loss of profits or injury to the debtor's business, the loss due to depreciation in value of the property, loss of use of the property, and the loss of interest. Damages for mental suffering may also be recoverable if caused by the wrongful garnishment or attachment. Many states also permit the debtor to recover the cost of attorney's fees and court costs.

#### Punitive Damages

The debtor may be entitled to punitive damages. Punitive damages are those damages awarded as a punishment against the wrongdoer, and are supposed to act as a deterrent against further wrongdoing. Punitive damages are usually awarded in actions where the attachment or garnishment, in addition to being wrongful, was also done maliciously, willfully and without probable cause. In other words, the attachment was issued for the purpose of harassing or oppressing the debtor, rather than to preserve legal rights. For example, punitive damages have been awarded in suits where the creditor attached exempt property, knowing the property was exempt.

## SECURED TRANSACTIONS

### In General

Secured transactions are governed by Article 9 of the *Uniform Commercial Code* (UCC). A secured transaction occurs when a lender (the secured party) and a borrower (the debtor) enter into a security agreement whereby the borrower gives the lender an interest in specific property owned by the borrower, known as collateral, if the borrower defaults on the loan. The security interest applies to any transaction that is intended to create a security interest in personal property. This interest allows the lender to provide financing or other assets to the borrower in order to further the purpose of the transaction.

### The Security Agreement

Unless the lender is in possession of the collateral pursuant to the agreement—i.e., the collateral is "pledged"—a security interest is not enforceable against the borrower or third parties, and cannot attach, until the borrower has signed a security agreement. The agreement to provide for a security interest must be in writing, signed by the borrower, and must describe the collateral.

The requirement of a writing is for evidentiary purposes in case a future conflict arises over the terms of the agreement and the identity of the collateral. Therefore, if the collateral is pledged, the need for a writing is of less importance and thus not required by the statute. Additional terms in a security agreement may include the amount of the debt and terms of repayment; and risk of loss and insurance provisions.

Value must be given in return for the security interest in order for it to attach. Value refers to any consideration sufficient to support a simple contract. For example: Buyer (borrower) purchases a washing machine from Seller (lender) on an installment basis. Buyer and Seller agree that Seller will retain a security interest in the washing machine in case Buyer reneges on the payments. The sale of the washing machine to Buyer is the consideration that supports the contract.

A pledged security agreement exists when the borrower transfers the collateral to the secured party in exchange for a loan. An example of a pledged security agreement would be where the borrower leaves an item with a pawnbroker in return for a cash payment and the borrower retains the right to redeem the item.

### Risk of Loss

If the lender is in possession of the collateral, he or she is required to use reasonable care in preserving the collateral. However, the obligation to pay reasonable expenses is chargeable to the borrower, and also secured by the collateral. A type of such expense is insurance coverage. Thus, the risk of accidental loss or damage to the collateral is borne by the borrower if there is insufficient insurance coverage.

### Default

If the borrower defaults on the security agreement, the lender can regain possession of the property. Whether a debtor is in default depends on the terms of the security agreement. For example, an agreement will invariably provide that failure to make payments required under the agreement constitutes default.

In addition to any rights and remedies provided in the security agreement in case of default, Article 9 affords the secured party further relief. For example, the secured party may execute against—i.e., reduce the claim to judgment and request the sheriff to levy—the debtor's property, which is then sold and the proceeds applied to the debt. If the agreement covers both real and personal property, the lender may foreclose on the real property.

In addition, the secured party may take possession of the collateral, if it is not already in his possession, or may sell the collateral and apply the proceeds of the sale to satisfy the claim. Of course, if there is any deficiency—an amount still owing after the sale proceeds have been applied to the debt—after the sale, the debtor is still liable for the deficiency. The lender must also account to the debtor for any surplus proceeds resulting from a sale of the collateral.

If the borrower files for bankruptcy, the security interest provides the lender with assurance that he or she may be able to recover the value of the loan by taking possession of the specified collateral.

### Redemption

At any time before the lender has disposed of the collateral, the borrower may redeem the collateral by fulfilling the obligations secured by the collateral, as well as reimbursing the lender for any expenses reasonably incurred in connection with the borrower's default. This may include legal fees and costs.

If the lender wants to retain the collateral in full satisfaction of the borrower's obligation, written notice of the lender's intent must be

## JUDGMENT ENFORCEMENT

sent to the borrower unless the borrower has already stated they were giving up their rights in the collateral. If the borrower does not object to the lender's notice, the lender may retain the collateral.

Because a security agreement is also a contract, it must comply with any other state laws governing contracts. Thus, the reader is advised to further check the law of his or her own jurisdiction when researching a specific issue.

# CHAPTER 7: CONSUMER BANKRUPTCY

**IN GENERAL**

If the debtor's financial situation is so bad that there is no hope of getting out of debt, he or she may consider the option of filing bankruptcy. The bankruptcy laws were enacted to give an honest debtor a "fresh start" in life by relieving the debtor of most debts, and to repay creditors in an orderly manner to the extent that the debtor has property available for payment. Individuals have a choice in deciding which chapter of the Bankruptcy Code best suits their needs. The serious decision of whether to file for bankruptcy, and under which chapter, depends on the financial circumstances of the particular individual.

**EXPLORING THE ALTERNATIVES**

It is recommended that the individual considering bankruptcy obtain competent legal advice before proceeding. All available alternatives should be explored to make certain that there are no less drastic solutions that would solve the individual's financial problems. This is particularly so when the debtor's liabilities are primarily consumer debt, such as credit card obligations, and the individual is basically "judgment proof"—i.e., he or she has little or no income or assets from which recovery can be made—and no major changes to this scenario are anticipated. In such a case, the individual can simply "walk away" because the creditor can't attach any property.

An individual can also try to deal with the creditors directly and work out a new payment plan. Creditors generally prefer working out a payment arrangement rather than pursuing legal methods of debt recovery. Often, the cooperative approach is more likely to result in payments being made.

Nevertheless, even if an individual is being harassed by collection agencies, it is still not necessary to immediately file for bankruptcy protection. As further discussed in this almanac, the consumer is entitled to certain protection under state and federal law to stop debt collection harassment. For example, debt collectors are legally prohibited from using deceitful or threatening tactics. Further, they are legally prohibited from contacting an individual once they are given written notice that all contact should cease.

Other than telephoning and writing the debtor to request payment, a creditor has no legal right to collect on a debt unless the creditor sues the debtor and obtains a judgment. Thus, if debt collection efforts fail, a creditor has to make a decision whether it is financially wise to start a lawsuit to recover the debt. It would be virtually impossible for creditors to sue all of the consumers who fail to pay their debts. The legal fees, costs and the time it takes to obtain a judgment would likely far outweigh any recovery the creditor could expect. Often the creditor will take the uncollected debt and write it off as a cost of doing business—known as a "charge-off"—after a period of time.

Of course, this causes considerable damage to the debtor's credit rating for approximately seven years, but collection action usually ends, and a lawsuit is not likely initiated to recover the debt. Once the applicable statute of limitations has expired, the creditor is legally prevented from filing a lawsuit against the debtor.

In considering whether to charge off the debt, or to take legal action, the creditor generally weighs a number of factors, including whether the debtor is judgment proof. If the creditor does decide to sue, and obtains a judgment against the debtor, the creditor must then attempt to collect the judgment amount from the debtor's property and/or income.

There are exemption laws, however, which protect much of the debtor's property from collection. Also, any property that is not protected must be significant for the creditor to pursue collection, because of the attendant costs of seizing and selling the property, e.g. sheriff's poundage charges.

If the creditor places a lien on the debtor's home, unless the lien is a considerable amount, it is not likely that the creditor will foreclose on the debtor's home to collect the debt. The costs of foreclosure are substantial, and the creditor generally stands in line behind the mortgage holder, taxing authorities and any previously filed liens before getting paid, if at all. It is more likely that the creditor will wait until the debtor chooses to sell or refinance his or her home, at which time the debt must be paid at or before closing to transfer clear title to the property.

As further discussed in this almanac, creditors are more apt to go after a debtor's wages or other income to collect on a judgment. However, public benefits, such as unemployment, public assistance, disability, or social security benefits are generally protected. Also, if there is income—such as wages or pension and retirement benefits—eligible to satisfy a judgment, there are laws that limit the amount that can be taken at any given time.

Finally, an individual can contact one of the many debt consolidation and credit counseling services that specialize in consumer credit problems to discuss other less drastic ways to resolve their debts.

Thus, consumer debt need not be the catalyst to an immediate bankruptcy filing. If the debtor doesn't have a significant source of steady income, or property that is secured by the debt—e.g., a mortgage or automobile loan—bankruptcy may not be necessary.

### ADVANTAGES AND DISADVANTAGES OF FILING BANKRUPTCY

Bankruptcy is a serious step which may have certain relatively long-term consequences. One must carefully assess his or her financial situation and determine whether bankruptcy is the right course to take given all of the advantages and disadvantages.

Filing bankruptcy gives the debtor some time to rethink his or her financial situation without worrying about a foreclosure sale of his or her home due to mortgage arrears or tax debts. The automatic stay, which is further discussed below, prevents all creditors from taking any legal action against the debtor once the bankruptcy petition has been filed.

In addition, bankruptcy provides a new start to individuals who are saddled with consumer debt that they are unable to repay. Credit card debt is particularly difficult to resolve. It is not uncommon for the balance on a credit card account to actually increase despite years of payment and non-use. This is because the monthly finance charge cancels out a significant portion of the monthly payment, and added late charges and overlimit charges may greatly increase the amount owed.

Bankruptcy provides the debtor a legal method to wipe out a significant amount—if not all—of his or her debts. The debtor is given the opportunity to manage his or her financial affairs without this burden. Generally, there is no minimum amount of debt necessary to file for bankruptcy.

The most apparent disadvantage of filing for bankruptcy protection is the serious damage inflicted on the debtor's credit rating. A bankruptcy filing can remain on an individual's credit report for 10 years under the provisions of the Fair Credit Reporting Act. Under the law, a credit reporting agency may not report a bankruptcy case on a person's credit report after ten years from the date the bankruptcy case is filed.

If a chapter 13 bankruptcy is successfully completed, the credit reporting industry generally retains the information for only seven years rather than the ten years allowed by law. This is a policy decision made in order to encourage individuals to opt for debt repayment under chapter 13 rather than liquidation under chapter 7.

This negative credit information generally impedes any efforts to obtain credit, e.g. for a home or automobile purchase, for a considerable period of time. However, an individual who is in debt to the degree that he or she is considering filing bankruptcy has more than likely already sustained considerable damage to his or her credit.

Nevertheless, the decision whether to grant an individual credit in the future is strictly up to the creditor and varies from creditor to creditor depending on the type of credit requested. There is no law that prevents anyone from extending credit to a debtor immediately after the filing of a bankruptcy nor will a creditor be required to extend credit.

Another disadvantage to filing bankruptcy is that the bankruptcy petition, schedules and other filings are a matter of public record. The debtor must disclose all of his or her personal financial information for at least the previous two years, and all of this information is available for public scrutiny. In chapter 13 cases, the debtor's employer may also be involved because this chapter may require deductions from the debtor's paycheck as part of the debt repayment plan.

In addition, co-signers do not benefit from the discharge obtained by a chapter 7 debtor. Therefore, if a friend or relative co-signed a loan for the debtor, they will be left wholly responsible for repayment of the debt unless they also file bankruptcy. However, in chapter 13, the co-signer cannot be pursued for the debt if the debtor agrees to pay the debt in full, remains in chapter 13, and continues to make payments to the creditor.

### COMMENCING THE BANKRUPTCY CASE

If you have weighed all of your options, and considered the advantages and disadvantages of filing for bankruptcy, and it appears that filing for bankruptcy protection is your best course of action for dealing with your debts, you must decide whether you want to file your case under chapter 13 (debt adjustment) or chapter 7 (liquidation) of the bankruptcy code.

Debtor's voluntary petition (Official Form 1) is set forth at Appendix 14 of this almanac.

### Chapter 13 – Individual Debt Adjustment

Any individual is eligible to file for chapter 13 bankruptcy relief as long as their debts do not exceed a certain monetary limit. Presently, the statutory maximum is $307,675 in unsecured debts, and $922,975 in secured debts. These limits are adjusted periodically to reflect changes in the consumer price index.

A chapter 13 bankruptcy case is also referred to as a "wage earner's plan" because it enables debtors who have a regular income to develop a repayment plan under which creditors are paid over a period ranging from three to five years.

As further discussed below, when a chapter 13 petition is filed, the debtor receives an "automatic stay" that stops most collection actions against the debtor or the debtor's property. In addition to the automatic stay, there are a number of advantages to filing a bankruptcy petition under chapter 13 instead of pursuing liquidation under chapter 7.

One major reason an individual may wish to file under chapter 13 is to keep their home from being foreclosed upon by their home mortgage lender if they fall behind in their payments. Chapter 13 allows the debtor to stop foreclosure proceedings pursuant to the automatic stay provision, and pay any past due amount over an extended period of time. However, current mortgage payments must be timely made while the chapter 13 case is pending.

Another advantage to filing under chapter 13 is the ability to reschedule secured debts—i.e., those debts for which the creditor has the right to take certain property pledged as "collateral"—and extend debt repayment over the duration of the chapter 13 repayment plan. This generally results in lower payments. In addition, the repayment plan may offer creditors less than the full payment on their claims. The repayment plan must be submitted for court approval, also known as "confirmation."

A chapter 13 debtor makes his or her plan payments in a lump sum to the case trustee who then distributes the payments to the creditors pursuant to the debtor's repayment plan. The debtor no longer has contact with his or her creditors.

A sample Chapter 13 Repayment Plan is set forth at Appendix 15 of this almanac.

If the debtor does not make the required payments under the repayment plan, the debtor's chapter 13 case may be dismissed by the court, or converted into a liquidation case under chapter 7 of the Bankruptcy Code, as discussed below.

### Chapter 7—Liquidation

A chapter 7 bankruptcy case involves the "liquidation" of the debtor's assets. Like a chapter 13 case, when a chapter 7 petition is filed, the debtor receives an "automatic stay" that stops most collection actions against the debtor or the debtor's property, although depending on the debtor's situation, the stay may be short-lived. The automatic stay provision is discussed more fully below.

Unlike chapter 13, eligibility for filing for chapter 7 bankruptcy relief does not depend on the amount of debt involved, or whether the debtor is solvent or insolvent. However, if an individual debtor's current monthly income is more than the state median income, the Bankruptcy Code requires the application of the "means test" to determine whether the chapter 7 filing is presumptively abusive.

Presently, under the law, abuse is presumed if the debtor's aggregate current monthly income over 5 years, net of certain statutorily allowed expenses, is more than: (i) $10,000, or (ii) 25% of the debtor's nonpriority unsecured debt, as long as that amount is at least $6,000.

The debtor may rebut this presumption of abuse by showing special circumstances that justify additional expenses or adjustments of current monthly income. Unless the debtor overcomes the presumption of abuse, the case will either be dismissed, or converted to chapter 13 with the debtor's consent.

### Administration of a Chapter 7 Bankruptcy Case

A chapter 7 debtor does not propose a debt repayment plan like a chapter 13 debtor. In administering a chapter 7 case, the case trustee gathers and sells all of the debtor's nonexempt assets and uses the proceeds to pay the creditors. Although a chapter 7 debtor is permitted to keep certain property that is deemed exempt under the law, the trustee will liquidate all of the debtor's remaining assets. The creditors are paid from the nonexempt property of the estate, if any. Thus, if you are considering filing a chapter 7 case, you should be aware that this will likely result in the loss of your property.

A table of federal exemptions is set forth at Appendix 16 and a table of state exemptions is set forth at Appendix 17 of this almanac.

If the debtor has no assets, or all of the debtor's assets are exempt or subject to valid liens, the trustee will file a "no-asset" report with the court, and there will be no distribution to unsecured creditors. If there are assets, the case trustee liquidates the debtor's nonexempt assets by selling the debtor's property provided: (i) the property is either free and clear of liens; or (ii) the property is worth more than any security interest or lien attached to it; or (iii) the property is worth more than any exempt amount the debtor holds in the property.

In order to make a claim, a creditor files a written statement known as a "proof of claim." The proof of claim sets forth the details of the creditor's claim and should include a copy of the obligation giving rise to the claim. If the claim is secured, the creditor should also provide evidence of the secured status. The debtor is entitled to object to any claim filed in their bankruptcy case if they believe the debt is not owed, or if they dispute the amount or kind of debt claimed.

A sample Proof of Claim is set forth at Appendix 18 of this almanac.

A Statement of Intention is a form filed in a Chapter 7 case which provides the court with information concerning the debtors intentions relating to assets which secure debts, such as the debtor's home or car. The debtor must disclose whether he or she intends to retain the asset or surrender it. If the debtor wishes to keep the asset, he or she must continue to pay for it. An agreement may be reached with the creditor for payment. This agreement must be in writing and may require approval by the bankruptcy judge. The debtor generally has two options for payment of the debt, as discussed below.

### Reaffirmation Agreement

If a debtor wants to keep certain property that is secured by a lien, such as their car, he or she may enter into a reaffirmation agreement with the secured creditor. The reaffirmation agreement must be filed with the court. If the debtor is not represented by an attorney, the bankruptcy judge must approve the reaffirmation agreement.

Under a reaffirmation agreement, the debtor and creditor agree that the debtor will remain liable for the debt even though the debt would otherwise be discharged in bankruptcy and the debtor would no longer be personally liable. The creditor promises that it will not repossess the secured property, e.g., the car, as long as the debtor continues to pay the debt.

Under the law, a reaffirmation agreement must contain certain disclosures. For example, the agreement must advise the debtor of the following: (i) the amount of the debt being reaffirmed; (ii) how the amount was calculated; (iii) that the debtor will continue to be personally liable for the debt; and (iv) that the debt will not be discharged.

The law also requires the debtor to sign a statement of his or her current income and expenses which shows that the debtor has a sufficient balance of income to pay the reaffirmed debt. If the balance is not enough to pay the debt to be reaffirmed, there is a presumption of undue hardship, in which case the court may refuse to approve the reaffirmation agreement.

A sample Reaffirmation Agreement (Form B240) is set forth at Appendix 19 of this almanac.

It should be noted, however, that a debtor may repay any debt voluntarily regardless of whether a reaffirmation agreement exists.

### Redemption

An alternative to reaffirmation is redemption of property. The debtor may redeem certain property by agreeing to pay the creditor the full current value of the property in one lump sum, even if the debt is considerably higher. Property that may be redeemed generally includes tangible personal property intended for personal, family or household use, on which a lien has been filed. In addition, if the bankruptcy trustee abandons a piece of property from the bankruptcy estate, the debtor generally has the right to redeem that property as well.

### The Automatic Stay

Upon filing a bankruptcy petition, the debtor is afforded certain protections. The most significant of these protections is the automatic stay. The automatic stay prevents the debtor's creditors from taking any further action to collect debts while the bankruptcy case is pending. The purpose of the automatic stay is to take some of the pressure off of the debtor by allowing him or her to work within the bankruptcy system to manage their financial debt, without having to simultaneously deal with creditors.

In order to fully take advantage of the automatic stay, the debtor should immediately notify all of his or her creditors instead of waiting for the court to make the notification. Anyone who violates the automatic stay by continuing to pursue legal action may be held in contempt of court and suffer penalties as a result.

In general, the automatic stay suspends the following types of action:

1. Wage garnishment;

2. Foreclosure;

3. Eviction or utility service suspension;

4. Automobile repossession; and

5. Lawsuits based upon failure to pay a debt that are pending or that could have been filed prior to the bankruptcy filing.

### Exceptions to the Automatic Stay

There are certain exceptions to the automatic stay that have been put into place by legislation and/or the judiciary. Examples of such exceptions include but are not limited to the following:

1. The commencement or continuation of criminal proceedings against the debtor are not subject to the stay. In criminal proceedings that involve both a crime and a debt, the automatic stay will only serve to suspend that portion of the proceedings that involves payment of the debt. For example, if an individual is convicted of criminal mischief for breaking a window, and is sentenced to fifteen days in jail and restitution for the cost of the window, a bankruptcy filing may stay payment of the restitution amount, but won't affect the incarceration.

2. The commencement or continuation of collection actions for alimony, maintenance or support, from property that is not property of the bankruptcy estate, is not subject to the stay. Further, paternity actions and lawsuits seeking to establish, modify or enforce child support or alimony, are not stayed by a bankruptcy filing.

3. Taxing authorities may be stayed from filing a tax lien or seizing the debtor's property, however, they may continue to conduct audits, demand tax returns, and issue tax assessments and demands for payment of the assessed tax.

4. The commencement or enforcement of any action by a governmental unit under its police powers that generally concerns public health and safety, and environmental and related matters, is not subject to the stay.

5. If a lease or other tenancy for nonresidential real estate was terminated by the landlord prior to the bankruptcy filing, the landlord may continue to enforce its rights to obtain possession despite the stay.

### Violating the Automatic Stay

If a creditor continues to attempt to collect a debt after the bankruptcy petition is filed in violation of the automatic stay, the debtor should immediately notify the creditor in writing that they have filed for bankruptcy protection. The letter should include the case name, number, and filing date, or a copy of the petition that shows it was filed.

If, despite these efforts, the creditor still continues to try to collect, the debtor may be entitled to take legal action against the creditor to obtain a specific order from the court prohibiting the creditor from taking further collection action. If the creditor is willfully violating the automatic stay, the court can hold the creditor in contempt of court and punish the creditor by fine or incarceration.

Because any such legal action brought against the creditor will likely be complex, obtaining legal representation by a qualified bankruptcy attorney is advised.

### Obtaining Relief From the Automatic Stay

A creditor may want to proceed in their collection efforts against the debtor after a bankruptcy petition has been filed. Unless the action falls under an exception as set forth above, a creditor must make a "Motion for Relief from the Automatic Stay" to the bankruptcy court to lift—i.e., remove—the stay as it pertains to that creditor. The motion generally requires a hearing before the Bankruptcy Judge at which time the creditor must demonstrate to the court that the stay is not serving its intended purpose.

For example, a debtor may file for bankruptcy protection to stop the foreclosure on his or her house. However, if it is determined that the debtor has no equity in the house—i.e., the amount of debt exceeds the fair market value of the house—and no way of repaying the arrears on the mortgage, the court may grant the mortgage holder's motion to lift the automatic stay. This enables the secured creditor to proceed with the foreclosure and sale of the property.

The creditor may also request the debtor to agree to a "Stipulation for Relief from the Automatic Stay," in order to avoid a formal hearing.

### The Effect of Property Abandonment on The Automatic Stay

If the bankruptcy trustee who is administering the bankruptcy estate believes that there is no equity in certain property of the estate, the trustee may "abandon" the property. That is because the trustee's duty is to sell assets in order to create a fund from which creditors will be repaid. A piece of property in which the debtor has no equity will add nothing to this fund.

When a particular piece of property is abandoned by the trustee it is no longer protected under the automatic stay and the creditors who hold mortgages or liens against the particular piece of property are free to proceed legally to recover the property. It is no longer protected under the automatic stay.

### Discharged Debts

A bankruptcy discharge is an order that releases the debtor from personal liability for certain types of debts. Once the debtor receives the discharge, the debtor is no longer legally responsible for those debts, and creditors can no longer take any collection action against the debtor for those discharged debts.

A sample bankruptcy discharge order is set forth at Appendix 20 of this almanac.

If a creditor continues collection efforts, the debtor can file a motion with the bankruptcy court. The bankruptcy court will generally reopen the case to handle the creditor's violation of the discharge order. The court can find the creditor in contempt of court, and assess a fine against the creditor as punishment for violating the discharge order.

Nevertheless, if there is a valid lien upon specific property that secured the debt, the secured creditor can still enforce the lien to recover the property secured by the lien unless the lien has been "avoided"—made unenforceable—in the bankruptcy case. Although a debtor is no longer personally responsible for a discharged debt, he or she may still voluntarily repay the debt. This may occur, for example, if the debtor wishes to keep the property that is subject to a lien, or when a debt is owed to a family member.

### The Debtor's Right to a Discharge of Debts

The bankruptcy discharge given to the debtor varies depending on the bankruptcy chapter—generally either chapter 7 or 13—under which the debtor files his or her case.

### Chapter 7 Cases

In a chapter 7 case, the debtor does not have an absolute right to a discharge. Any creditor, the U.S. trustee, or the case trustee, may file an objection to the debtor's discharge. Shortly after the case is filed, creditors receive a notice that advises them of the deadline for making an objection to the discharge. If a creditor chooses to object, he or she must file a complaint in the bankruptcy court before this deadline. The filing of the complaint starts a litigation process known as an "adversary proceeding." At trial, the objecting party has the burden of proving all of the facts essential to their objection.

The court may deny a chapter 7 discharge for any of the reasons set forth in the Bankruptcy Code (Section 727(a)), including:

1. Failure to provide requested tax documents;

2. Failure to complete a course on personal financial management;

3. Transfer or concealment of property with intent to hinder, delay, or defraud creditors;

4. Destruction or concealment of books or records;

5. Perjury and other fraudulent acts;

6. Failure to account for the loss of assets; or

In addition, the court will deny a discharge in a later chapter 7 case if the debtor received a discharge under chapter 7 or chapter 11 in a case filed within eight years before the second petition is filed. The court will also deny a chapter 7 discharge if the debtor previously received a discharge in a chapter 12 or chapter 13 case filed within six years before the date of the filing of the second case unless: (i) the debtor paid all "allowed unsecured" claims in the earlier case in full, or (ii) the debtor made payments under the plan in the earlier case totaling at least 70 percent of the allowed unsecured claims, and the debtor's plan was proposed in good faith and the payments represented the debtor's best effort.

The court usually grants the discharge promptly following expiration of: (i) the time fixed for filing objections to the discharge; and (ii) the time fixed for filing a motion to dismiss the case for substantial abuse, i.e. 60 days following the first date set for the meeting of creditors ("the 341 meeting"). In general, this occurs about four months after the date the debtor files his or her bankruptcy petition.

### Chapter 13 Cases

In a chapter 13 case, the debtor is usually entitled to a discharge upon completion of all payments under the plan. However, a debtor who fails to complete the required course on personal financial management may be denied a discharge. The debtor is ineligible for discharge under chapter 13 if he or she received a prior discharge in a chapter 7, 11, or 12 case filed four years before the current case or in a chapter 13 case filed two years before the current case.

The court usually grants the discharge as soon as practicable after the debtor completes all payments under their repayment plan. A chapter 13 plan may provide for payments to be made over three to five years, therefore, the discharge typically occurs about four years after the date of filing.

There are some limited circumstances under which the debtor may request the court to grant a "hardship discharge" even though the debtor has failed to complete plan payments due to circumstances beyond the debtor's control.

### Nondischargeable Debts

Certain debts cannot be discharged, and the types of debts discharged vary depending on the type of case filed. There are nineteen categories of nondischargeable debts under chapters 7 and a more limited list of nondischargeable debts under chapter 13. The debtor must still pay those nondischargeable debts after bankruptcy.

The most common types of debts which are automatically deemed nondischargeable include:

1. Certain types of tax claims;

2. Debts not listed by the debtor on the schedules the debtor must file with the court;

3. Debts for spousal or child support or alimony;

4. Debts for willful and malicious injuries to person or property;

5. Debts to governmental units for fines and penalties;

6. Debts for most government funded or guaranteed educational loans or benefit overpayments;

7. Debts for personal injury caused by the debtor's operation of a motor vehicle while intoxicated;

8. Debts owed to certain tax-advantaged retirement plans; and

9. Debts for certain condominium or cooperative housing fees.

Certain other types of debts, such as obligations affected by fraud or maliciousness, are not automatically deemed nondischargeable. In those cases, the creditor must ask the court to determine whether the debt is nondischargeable. However, if a creditor does not request a determination by the court, the debt will be discharged.

Under chapter 13, a debtor receives a broader discharge of debts. For example, debts dischargeable in a chapter 13, but not in chapter 7, include:

1. Debts for willful and malicious injury to property;

2. Debts incurred to pay nondischargeable tax obligations; and

3. Debts arising from property settlements in divorce or separation proceedings.

### Revoking a Bankruptcy Discharge

The court may revoke a discharge under certain circumstances. For example, a creditor, the U.S. trustee, or the case trustee, may request that the court revoke the debtor's discharge in a chapter 7 case based on certain allegations, including:

1. The debtor obtained the discharge fraudulently;

2. The debtor failed to disclose the fact that he or she acquired or became entitled to acquire property that would constitute property of

the bankruptcy estate; committed one of several acts of impropriety described in section 727(a)(6) of the *Bankruptcy Code*; or failed to explain any misstatements discovered in an audit of the case or fails to provide documents or information requested in an audit of the case. Typically, a request to revoke the debtor's discharge must be filed within one year of the discharge or, in some cases, before the date that the case is closed. The court will decide whether such allegations are true and, if so, whether to revoke the discharge. In a chapter 13 case, if confirmation of a plan or the discharge is obtained through fraud, the court can revoke the order of confirmation or discharge.

A more detailed discussion of bankruptcy laws and procedures may be found in this author's legal almanac entitled Individual Bankruptcy published by Oceana Publishing Company.

A directory of U.S. Bankruptcy Courts is set forth at Appendix 21 of this almanac.

# CHAPTER 8:
# REHABILITATING YOUR CREDIT

**WHAT IS A CREDIT REPORT?**

When a consumer applies for credit, such as a credit card or an automobile loan, he or she generally fills out an application form which sets forth information concerning the consumer's creditworthiness. In considering the application, the creditor generally requests a report from a credit reporting agency to: (i) verify the information; (ii) obtain additional information concerning the consumer's ability to take on additional debt; (iii) obtain the consumer's credit payment history, e.g. whether the consumer pays debts timely or late; and (iv) determine whether there are any unpaid judgments or liens against the consumer that would affect their creditworthiness.

The three major credit reporting agencies listed below regularly obtain information from creditors concerning the payment history of its customers. They also search public records for judgment and lien information. When you are unable to pay your debts on time, late payments and other adverse action—such as judgments and liens—will appear on your credit report.

**REQUESTING YOUR CREDIT REPORT**

In order to begin rehabilitating your credit, you need to find out all of the information the credit reporting agencies maintain in your credit file, as well as your credit score. You can now order your credit reports from all three credit reporting agencies online. Contact information for the three major national credit bureaus is as follows:

EQUIFAX
P.O. Box 740241
Atlanta, GA 30374
Tel: (800) 685-1111
Website: www.equifax.com

EXPERIAN
701 Experian Parkway
Allen, TX 75013
Tel: (888) 397-3742
Website: www.experian.com

TRANS UNION
P.O. Box 1000
Chester, PA 19022
Tel: (800) 916-8800
Website: www.transunion.com

### The FACT Act

The *Fair and Accurate Credit Transactions (FACT) Act* was signed into law in December 2003. The FACT Act added new sections to the federal Fair Credit Reporting Act (15 U.S.C. 1681 et seq.).

#### Free Annual Disclosure Provision

Among other provisions, the FACT Act entitles a consumer to receive a free copy of a consumer disclosure every 12 months from Equifax, Experian, and TransUnion, the three major credit reporting agencies.

If you live in one of the seven states that had laws requiring the credit reporting agencies to provide consumers with a free credit report annually prior to passage of the FACT Act, you can obtain a free credit report under your state's law in addition to the report you are entitled to under federal law. Those seven states are Colorado, Georgia, Maine, Maryland, Massachusetts, New Jersey, and Vermont.

A consumer disclosure refers to all the information in a consumer's credit report that the credit reporting agencies maintain, including information about everyone who has received information from the credit reporting agencies about the consumer's credit file, i.e., inquiries. A consumer disclosure differs from a credit report in that a credit report contains only some of the information in your credit file.

Under the FACT Act, you are also entitled to receive this information at no charge if you certify to the credit reporting agency that:

1. You are unemployed and intend to apply for employment in the 60-day period beginning on the date you make the certification;

2. You receive public welfare assistance;

3. You believe your file contains inaccurate information due to fraud; or

4. You are a victim of identity theft.

You can request your FACT Act consumer disclosure from one or more of the three credit reporting agencies online, by telephone and by mail, as follows:

Online: Access the website at http://www.annualcreditreport.com/. Follow the instructions on the website.

By Telephone: Call 1-877-322-8228 to request your credit reports by phone. You will go through a simple verification process over the phone, and your reports will be mailed to you.

By Mail: Send your request to the following address:

Annual Credit Report Request Service
P.O. Box 105281
Atlanta, GA 30348-5281

**Your Credit Score**

A credit score—also known as a risk score—is an individual consumer's statistically derived numerical value used by a lender to predict the likelihood of certain credit behaviors, including default. Lenders often make credit granting decisions based upon your credit score. In addition to late payments, factors such as your credit card limits and the number of inquiries in your credit file can lower your credit score and lead to a denial of credit. Therefore, it is advisable to find out your credit score prior to applying for credit.

Until the FACT Act was enacted, consumers were not given access to their credit score, or the factors that go into determining the score. Under new FACT Act provisions, you may request your credit score, including an explanation of the factors that went into computing your score. The credit reporting agencies are entitled to charge a reasonable fee, as determined by the Federal Trade Commission (FTC), for providing you with this information.

The disclosure fee provisions of the FACT Act are set forth at Appendix 22.

**MONITOR YOUR CREDIT REPORT REGULARLY**

To prevent identity theft and keep your credit file up-to-date, it is important to monitor your credit report regularly for accuracy. Credit reporting agencies are obligated to make sure the information contained in a consumer's file is current. The rationale for this requirement is to give the consumer a chance to rehabilitate a negative credit history. Maintaining information in this manner is helpful to both the creditor and consumer provided it is accurate, and maintained in a manner so as to protect the consumer's privacy rights.

For example, the consumer must authorize the creditor to obtain his or her credit report. Unauthorized release of credit information may result in an action for invasion of the consumer's right to privacy. In addition, inaccurate information, such as negligently reporting the consumer as a late payer, may result in a defamation action. Nevertheless, both of these remedies have their shortcomings when applied to consumer actions.

### The *Fair Credit Reporting Act*

In response to the inadequacy of the common law remedies for unfair credit reporting activities, Congress enacted the *Fair Credit Reporting Act* (the "FCRA") in 1970 as Subchapter III of its *Consumer Credit Protection Act*. The FCRA preempts any state statutes that are inconsistent with its provisions.

Under the FCRA, creditors may only obtain a consumer's credit report for limited purposes, the most common of which are extension of credit or employment. In addition, a creditor may only request a credit report for the individual consumer involved in the transaction, and cannot obtain a spouse's credit report if the spouse is not a party to the transaction. It is a crime under the FCRA to obtain a consumer's credit report under false pretenses.

If the credit reporting agency willfully or negligently issues a report to a person who does not have a permissible purpose in obtaining the report, the agency is subject to civil liability. An individual credit reporting agency employee who knowingly and willingly issues the report may be subject to criminal sanctions.

The FCRA also requires credit reporting agencies to maintain accurate information, and to permit consumers to correct any inaccuracies found in their reports. However, a credit reporting agency is not subject to civil liability for inaccuracies contained in consumer credit reports provided they "follow reasonable procedures to assure maximum possible accuracy of the information..." Nevertheless, if the credit-reporting agency does not follow "reasonable procedures," they may be subject to liability.

A credit reporting agency is liable to the consumer for any actual damages suffered as a result of negligence. Actual damages generally include monetary losses and have also been held to include damages for mental anguish resulting from aggravation, embarrassment, humiliation and injury to reputation, etc. Further, if the violation is willful, punitive damages may also be available to the consumer.

### Identify Problems

In order to improve your credit rating, you should identify those areas that are causing you problems, e.g. your credit report indicates a history of late payments. If you often forget to make your payments on time, most lenders have automated payment options that will deduct the payment from your designated bank account in a timely manner. If you use an automated payment option, you will avoid late payment fees and negative information being added to your credit profile. If your credit score is low because you have large balances on your credit cards, make an effort to reduce your balances and pay off high interest credit cards.

### Dispute Erroneous Information

Make sure all of your personal information is correct on your report, including your name, address, social security number, date of birth, employer, etc. Sometimes credit data get placed on the wrong report up, especially if you have a common name, e.g. Mary Jones. This often happens with family members who have the same name, such as John Smith, Sr. and John Smith, Jr.

You should dispute erroneous negative information in your credit report immediately. If you notice any strange item on your report, such as an unauthorized credit card, investigate it immediately. The FACT Act emphasizes the importance of accuracy in consumer credit files.

If the consumer disputes the accuracy of information contained in his or her file, the credit reporting agency is required to reinvestigate this information within a reasonable period of time. If, upon reinvestigation, the information cannot be verified, or is proven inaccurate, it must be deleted, and corrected copies must be sent to all parties who recently requested copies of the report.

A sample letter to a credit reporting agency disputing information contained in a credit report is set forth at Appendix 23.

Previously, disputes about the accuracy of information in a credit report had to be made directly to the credit reporting agency. Under the new FACT Act provisions, a consumer may dispute inaccurate information directly with the company that reported the information, and the company is required to investigate your claim upon notice of the disputed item.

After you have submitted your dispute, you should re-check your credit in 30 to 60 days to see whether the errors were corrected. If not, continue to dispute the misinformation. If the creditor refuses to remove the negative information from your file, you are entitled to add a statement to each of your three credit reports explaining your position.

TransUnion has prepared a credit report checklist to assist consumers on improving their credit and boosting their credit score. The worksheet should be filled out every time you check your credit report so you can track your improvement over time.

A credit report checklist is set forth at Appendix 24 of this almanac.

### Inquiries

Another segment of the credit report that can affect your credit score is the inquiry section. An inquiry is placed in your credit file when someone checks your credit information. A person checking your credit report must have a legitimate business reason to do so, such as a creditor or lender.

If a lender checks your credit for the purposes of approving a credit application, this is called a "hard" inquiry. Too many hard inquiries on your credit report can lower your credit score because lenders may believe you are applying for too much credit and will accumulate debt beyond your ability to pay.

If you notice a hard inquiry on your credit report that you do not recognize, contact the business that made the inquiry for more information. If the inquiry was made in error, you can dispute it and have it removed from your credit report. You should also be aware that an unauthorized inquiry might be a warning sign that someone applied for credit in your name and that you could be an intended target for identity theft.

A "soft" inquiry is placed in your credit file when someone checks your credit for a reason other than a credit application, e.g., to determine your eligibility for pre-approved credit offers. A soft inquiry does not affect your credit score.

### Early Warning Notice

As an additional protection against identity theft, The FACT Act requires creditors to give consumers an "early warning" notice that could alert you to a potential problem. A financial institution that extends credit must send you a notice before or no later than 30 days after negative information—e.g., late payments, default, etc.—is furnished to a credit reporting agency.

## HOW LONG DOES NEGATIVE INFORMATION REMAIN IN A CREDIT REPORT?

Negative information can remain in your credit file for a number of years; however, there are expiration dates, as set forth below. Oftentimes, you will find that the credit reporting agency has not removed the negative items by the expiration date; therefore, you should take it upon yourself to review the applicable dates and contact the credit reporting agency if items remain beyond their expiration date.

### Bankruptcy

Bankruptcies generally remain on your credit report for 10 years from the date you filed your petition, however, if you filed under Chapter 13 (individual debt adjustment), the item may be removed after 7 years.

### Charged Off Accounts

If your account is delinquent and the credit reports it as a "charged off account," this item can remain on your credit report for 7 years.

### Closed Accounts

A delinquent closed account can remain on your credit report for 7 years from the date reported. A closed account that was timely paid can remain on your account for more than 7 years.

### Collection Accounts

If your account is in collection, it can remain on your credit report for 7 years starting 181 days from the most recent delinquent period preceding the collection action.

### Inquiries

Hard inquiries can remain on your credit report for up to 2 years. Soft inquiries do not appear on the copy of your credit report that is provided to companies authorized to check your credit.

### Judgments

Judgments generally remain on your credit report for 7 years from the filing date.

### Late Payments

If you are between 30 and 180 days late in your payment, this item can remain on your credit report for 7 years.

### Tax Liens

A unpaid city, county, state and/or federal tax lien can remain on your credit report indefinitely, however, once the lien is satisfied, it will remain on your credit report for 7 years from the date of payment.

## OBTAINING LEGAL SERVICES

At various stages of indebtedness, you may want to retain a lawyer. A lawyer can contact creditors and try to establish a payment plan that will work within the debtor's budget. A lawyer may also be able to settle a debt—even after it has become a judgment—for an amount considerably less than the original debt. Although you can attempt to negotiate a settlement on your own, an attorney letter generally receives a more immediate response.

If a creditor is assured that they will be paid in a lump sum payment, they are often willing to negotiate. The last thing the creditor wants is for the debtor to declare bankruptcy. Thereafter, the chance of recovering any part of the debt is slim or nonexistent.

You should also consult a lawyer if you if have been victimized by unscrupulous debt collection practices. As further discussed in Chapter 5, debtors have statutory and common-law rights to take legal action for debt collection harassment.

Finally, if a creditor serves you with legal papers, you should consult a lawyer immediately. A legal response must be made on your behalf in order to prevent a default judgment from being entered against you.

**CREDIT REPAIR SERVICES**

There are companies that claim they can re-establish a good credit rating for the debtor—for a fee—despite how bad one's credit may be. It is generally best to avoid any companies that claim the ability to turn a bad credit report into a good one. The companies who advertise that they can erase bad credit are generally in business to earn a profit by undertaking actions that the individual can handle on their own. For example, if one's credit report includes negative information that is outdated, or contains inaccurate information, the credit-reporting agency, by law, must correct the inaccuracy. It is not necessary to pay someone to have this information deleted. This can easily be handled by the individual.

If, however, the negative credit report reflects legitimately owed debts, neither the debtor nor a credit repair service would be able to convince a credit reporting agency, or creditor, to report otherwise. Only time, a conscientious effort, and a personal debt repayment plan can improve a poor credit record.

The companies that advertise credit repair services appeal to consumers with poor credit histories. They cannot repair credit and, in fact, their tactics may be illegal and may also engage the consumer in illegal activity, such as asking the consumer to make false statements on credit applications, and fraudulently misrepresenting the consumer's social security number.

According to the Federal Trade Commission, a consumer must be aware of companies that:

1. Want you to pay for credit repair services before any services are provided;

2. Do not tell you your legal rights and what you can do yourself for free;

3. Recommend that you not contact a credit bureau directly;

4. Suggest that you try to invent a "new" credit report by applying for an Employer Identification Number to use instead of your Social Security Number; or

5. Advise you to dispute all information in your credit report or take any action that seems illegal, such as creating a new credit identity.

If you follow illegal advice and commit fraud, you may be subject to prosecution such as mail or wire fraud if you use the mail or telephone to apply for credit and provide false information.

**The Credit Repair Organizations Act**

Under the Credit Repair Organizations Act, credit repair organizations must give the consumer a copy of the "Consumer Credit File Rights Under State and Federal Law" before they sign a contract with the company. In addition, they also must give the consumer a written contract that spells out all of their rights and obligations. The law contains specific protections. For example, a credit repair company cannot:

1. Make false claims about their services;

2. Charge the consumer until they have completed the promised services; or

3. Perform any services until they have your signature on a written contract and have completed a three-day waiting period. During this time, you can cancel the contract without paying any fees.

In addition, the contract must specify:

1. The payment terms for services, including their total cost;

2. A detailed description of the services to be performed;

3. How long it will take to achieve the results;

4. Any guarantees they offer; and

5. The company's name and business address.

The text of the Credit Repair Organizations Act is set forth at Appendix 25.

# APPENDIX 1: TABLE OF THE MOST COMMON FORECLOSURE METHODS, BY STATE

| STATE | SECURITY INSTRUMENT | TYPE OF FORECLOSURE | NOTICE | DEFICIENCY |
|---|---|---|---|---|
| Alabama | Mortgage | Nonjudicial | Publication | Allowed |
| Alaska | Trust Deed | Nonjudicial | Notice of Default | Allowed |
| Arizona | Trust Deed | Nonjudicial | Notice of Sale | Allowed |
| Arkansas | Mortgage | Judicial | Complaint | Allowed |
| California | Trust Deed | Nonjudicial | Notice of Default | Prohibited |
| Colorado | Trust Deed | Nonjudicial | Notice of Default | Allowed |
| Connecticut | Mortgage | Strict | Complaint | Allowed |
| Delaware | Mortgage | Judicial | Complaint | Allowed |
| District of Columbia | Trust Deed | Nonjudicial | Notice of Default | Allowed |
| Florida | Mortgage | Judicial | Complaint | Allowed |
| Georgia | Security Deed | Nonjudicial | Publication | Allowed |
| Hawaii | Mortgage | Nonjudicial | Publication | Allowed |
| Idaho | Trust Deed | Nonjudicial | Notice of Default | Allowed |
| Illinois | Mortgage | Judicial | Complaint | Allowed |
| Indiana | Mortgage | Judicial | Complaint | Allowed |
| Iowa | Mortgage | Judicial | Petition | Allowed |
| Kansas | Mortgage | Judicial | Complaint | Allowed |
| Kentucky | Mortgage | Judicial | Complaint | Allowed |
| Louisiana | Mortgage | Executory Foreclosure | Petition | Allowed |
| Maine | Mortgage | Judicial | Complaint | Allowed |
| Maryland | Trust Deed | Nonjudicial | Notice | Allowed |

# TABLE OF THE MOST COMMON FORECLOSURE METHODS, BY STATE

| Massachusetts | Mortgage | Judicial | Complaint | Allowed |
|---|---|---|---|---|
| Michigan | Mortgage | Nonjudicial | Publication | Allowed |
| Minnesota | Mortgage | Nonjudicial | Publication | Prohibited |
| Missouri | Trust Deed | Nonjudicial | Publication | Allowed |
| Montana | Trust Deed | Nonjudicial | Notice | Prohibited |
| Nebraska | Mortgage | Judicial | Petition | Allowed |
| Nevada | Trust Deed | Nonjudicial | Notice of Default | Allowed |
| New Hampshire | Mortgage | Nonjudicial | Notice of Sale | Allowed |
| New Jersey | Mortgage | Judicial | Complaint | Allowed |
| New Mexico | Mortgage | Judicial | Complaint | Allowed |
| New York | Mortgage | Judicial | Complaint | Allowed |
| North Carolina | Trust Deed | Nonjudicial | Notice Hearing | Allowed |
| North Dakota | Mortgage | Judicial | Complaint | Prohibited |
| Ohio | Mortgage | Judicial | Complaint | Allowed |
| Oklahoma | Mortgage | Judicial | Complaint | Allowed |
| Oregon | Deed of Trust | Nonjudicial | Notice of Default | Prohibited |
| Pennsylvania | Mortgage | Judicial | Complaint | Allowed |
| Rhode Island | Mortgage | Nonjudicial | Publication | Allowed |
| South Carolina | Mortgage | Judicial | Complaint | Allowed |
| South Dakota | Mortgage | Judicial | Complaint | Allowed |
| Tennessee | Trust Deed | Nonjudicial | Publication | Allowed |
| Texas | Trust Deed | Nonjudicial | Publication | Allowed |
| Utah | Trust Deed | Nonjudicial | Notice of Default | Allowed |
| Vermont | Mortgage | Judicial | Complaint | Allowed |
| Virginia | Trust Deed | Nonjudicial | Publication | Allowed |
| Washington | Trust Deed | Nonjudicial | Notice of Default | Allowed |
| West Virginia | Trust Deed | Nonjudicial | Publication | Prohibited |
| Wisconsin | Mortgage | Judicial | Complaint | Allowed |
| Wyoming | Mortgage | Nonjudicial | Publication | Allowed |

# APPENDIX 2:
# TABLE OF STATE USURY LAWS

| STATE | LEGAL RATE | USURY LIMIT |
|---|---|---|
| ALABAMA | 6% | 8% |
| ALASKA | 10.5% | more than 5% above the Federal Reserve interest rate on the day the loan was made. |
| ARIZONA | 10% | n/a |
| ARKANSAS | 6% | 17% |
| CALIFORNIA | 10% | more than 5% greater than the rate of the Federal Reserve Bank of San Francisco (non-consumers) |
| COLORADO | 8% | 45% (general); 12% (consumers) |
| CONNECTICUT | 8% | 12% |
| DELAWARE | 5% over the Federal Reserve rate | n/a |
| DISTRICT OF COLUMBIA | 6% | 24% |
| FLORIDA | 12% | 18% (25% on loans above $500,000) |
| GEORGIA | 7% | 16% (loans below $3,000); 5% (loans above $3,000) |
| HAWAII | 10% | 12% (consumer transactions) |
| IDAHO | 12% | n/a |
| ILLINOIS | 5% | 9% |
| INDIANA | 10% | n/a |
| IOWA | 10% | 12% (consumer transactions) |
| KANSAS | 10% | 15% (general); 18% (consumer transactions-first $1,000); 14.45% (above $1,000) |
| KENTUCKY | 8% | 4% greater than the Federal Reserve rate or 19%, whichever is greater; no limit (loans above $15,000) |
| LOUISIANA | one point over the average prime rate | not to exceed 14% nor be less than 7%, 12% (individuals); no limit (corporations) |
| MAINE | 6% | n/a |

**Dealing with Debt**

# TABLE OF STATE USURY LAWS

| STATE | LEGAL RATE | USURY LIMIT |
|---|---|---|
| MARYLAND | 6% | 24% |
| MASSACHUSETTS | 6% | 20% (general) |
| MICHIGAN | 5% | 7% (general) |
| MINNESOTA | 6% | 8% |
| MISSISSIPPI | 9% | more than 10% or more than 5% above federal reserve rate; no limit (commercial loans above $5,000) |
| MISSOURI | 9% | no usury defense for corporations |
| MONTANA | 10% | above 6% greater than NYC bank prime rate |
| NEBRASKA | 6% | 16% (general) |
| NEVADA | 12% | no usury limit |
| NEW HAMPSHIRE | 10% | no usury limit |
| NEW JERSEY | 6% | 30% (individuals); 50% (corporations) |
| NEW MEXICO | 15% | n/a |
| NEW YORK | 9% | 16% (general) |
| NORTH CAROLINA | 8% | 8% (general) |
| NORTH DAKOTA | 6% | 5-1/2% above the six-month treasury bill interest rate. |
| OKLAHOMA | 6% | 10% (unless person is licensed to make consumer loans); 45% (non-consumer loans) |
| OREGON | 9% | 12% (loans below $50,000; 5% above discount rate (commercial paper) |
| PENNSYLVANIA | 6% | 6% (general for loans below $50,000 except loans with a lien on non-residential real estate; loans to corporations; loans that have no collateral above $35,000 |
| PUERTO RICO | 6% | as set by Finance Board of Office of Commissioner of Financial Institutions |
| RHODE ISLAND | 12% | 21% (general); 9% (T-Bills) |
| SOUTH CAROLINA | 8.75% | no usury limit subject to federal criminal laws against loan sharking |
| SOUTH DAKOTA | 15% | no usury limit |
| TENNESSEE | 10% | 24% or four points above average prime loan rate whichever is less |
| TEXAS | 6% | n/a |
| UTAH | 10% | floating rates (consumer transactions) |
| VERMONT | 12% | 12% (general); 18% (retail installment contracts-first $500); 15% (retail installment contracts-above $500) |

# TABLE OF STATE USURY LAWS

| STATE | LEGAL RATE | USURY LIMIT |
|---|---|---|
| VIRGINIA | 8% | multiple regulated rates (consumer loans); no usury limit (corporations and business loans); exempt (loans over $5,000 for business or investment purposes) |
| WASHINGTON | 12% | 12% (general) the legal rate is 12% or four points above the average T-Bill rate for the past 26 weeks whichever is greater. |
| WEST VIRGINIA | 6% | 8% (contractual rate), Commissioner of Banking issues rates (real estate loans) |
| WISCONSIN | 5% | no general usury limit (corporations), the legal rate of interest is 5% |
| WYOMING | 10% | n/a |

# APPENDIX 3
# INSTALLMENT AGREEMENT REQUEST

---

**Form 9465**
(Rev. November 2005)
Department of the Treasury
Internal Revenue Service

**Installment Agreement Request**

▶ If you are filing this form with your tax return, attach it to the front of the return. Otherwise, see instructions.

OMB No. 1545-0074

**Caution:** *Do not file this form if you are currently making payments on an installment agreement. Instead, call 1-800-829-1040. If you are in bankruptcy or we have accepted your offer-in-compromise, see* **Bankruptcy or offer-in-compromise** *on page 2.*

1. Your first name and initial — Last name — Your social security number

   If a joint return, spouse's first name and initial — Last name — Spouse's social security number

   Your current address (number and street). If you have a P.O. box and no home delivery, enter your box number. — Apt. number

   City, town or post office, state, and ZIP code. If a foreign address, enter city, province or state, and country. Follow the country's practice for entering the postal code.

2. If this address is new since you filed your last tax return, check here ▶ ☐

3. ( ) Your home phone number — Best time for us to call
4. ( ) Your work phone number — Ext. — Best time for us to call
5. Name of your bank or other financial institution:
   Address
   City, state, and ZIP code
6. Your employer's name:
   Address
   City, state, and ZIP code

7. Enter the tax return for which you are making this request (for example, Form 1040) _____ ▶
8. Enter the tax year for which you are making this request (for example, 2005) _____ ▶
9. Enter the total amount you owe as shown on your tax return (or notice) _____ | 9
10. Enter the amount of any payment you are making with your tax return (or notice). See instructions | 10
11. Enter the amount you can pay each month. **Make your payments as large as possible to limit interest and penalty charges.** The charges will continue until you pay in full. | 11
12. Enter the date you want to make your payment each month. **Do not** enter a date later than the 28th ▶
13. If you want to make your payments by electronic funds withdrawal from your checking account, see the instructions and fill in lines 13a and 13b. This is the most convenient way to make your payments and it will ensure that they are made on time.

▶ a Routing number ☐☐☐☐☐☐☐☐☐
▶ b Account number ☐☐☐☐☐☐☐☐☐☐☐☐☐☐☐☐☐

I authorize the U.S. Treasury and its designated Financial Agent to initiate a monthly ACH electronic funds withdrawal entry to the financial institution account indicated for payments of my federal taxes owed, and the financial institution to debit the entry to this account. This authorization is to remain in full force and effect until I notify the U.S. Treasury Financial Agent to terminate the authorization. To revoke payment, I must contact the U.S. Treasury Financial Agent at **1-800-829-1040** no later than 7 business days prior to the payment (settlement) date. I also authorize the financial institutions involved in the processing of the electronic payments of taxes to receive confidential information necessary to answer inquiries and resolve issues related to the payments.

Your signature — Date — Spouse's signature. If a joint return, **both** must sign. — Date

## General Instructions

Section references are to the Internal Revenue Code.

### Purpose of Form

Use Form 9465 to request a monthly installment plan if you cannot pay the full amount you owe shown on your tax return (or on a notice we sent you). Generally, you can have up to 60 months to pay. In certain circumstances, you can have longer to pay or your agreement can be approved for an amount that is less than the amount of tax you owe. But before requesting an installment agreement, you should consider other less costly alternatives, such as a bank loan or credit card payment. If you have any questions about this request, call 1-800-829-1040.

If you do not wish to enter into an installment agreement on Form 9465, the IRS offers alternative payment options. Some of these options that you may qualify for are:

- 120 day extension to pay, and
- Payroll deduction installment ageement.

For information on these and other methods of payment, call 1-800-829-1040.

**Guaranteed installment agreement.** Your request for an installment agreement cannot be turned down if the tax you owe is not more than $10,000 and all three of the following apply.

For Privacy Act and Paperwork Reduction Act Notice, see page 3.   Cat. No. 14842Y   Form **9465** (Rev. 11-2005)

---

**Dealing with Debt**

# INSTALLMENT AGREEMENT REQUEST

- During the past 5 tax years, you (and your spouse if filing a joint return) have timely filed all income tax returns and paid any income tax due, and have not entered into an installment agreement for payment of income tax.
- The IRS determines that you cannot pay the tax owed in full when it is due and you give the IRS any information needed to make that determination.
- You agree to pay the full amount you owe within 3 years and to comply with the tax laws while the agreement is in effect.

⚠ **CAUTION** *A Notice of Federal Tax Lien may be filed to protect the government's interests until you pay in full.*

**Bankruptcy or offer-in-compromise.** If you are in bankruptcy or we have accepted your offer-in-compromise, do not file this form. Instead, call 1-800-829-1040 to get the number of your local IRS Insolvency function for bankruptcy or Technical Support function for offer-in-compromise.

## What Will You Be Charged

You will be charged a $43 fee if your request is approved. Do not include the fee with this form. After approving your request, we will bill you for the fee with your first payment.

You will also be charged interest and may be charged a late payment penalty on any tax not paid by its due date, even if your request to pay in installments is granted. Interest and any applicable penalties will be charged until the balance is paid in full. To limit interest and penalty charges, file your return on time and pay as much of the tax as possible with your return (or notice).

## How Does the Installment Agreement Work

If we approve your request, we will send you a letter. It will tell you how to pay the fee and make your first installment payment. We will usually let you know within 30 days after we receive your request whether it is approved or denied. But if this request is for tax due on a return you filed after March 31, it may take us longer than 30 days to reply.

By approving your request, we agree to let you pay the tax you owe in monthly installments instead of immediately paying the amount in full. All payments received will be applied to your account in the best interests of the United States. In return, you agree to make your monthly payments on time. You also agree to meet all your future tax liabilities. This means that you must have enough withholding or estimated tax payments so that your tax liability for future years is paid in full when you timely file your return. Your request for an installment agreement will be denied if all required tax returns have not been filed. Any refund due you in a future year will be applied against the amount you owe. If your refund is applied to your balance, you are still required to make your regular monthly installment payment.

After we receive each payment, we will send you a letter showing the remaining amount you owe, and the due date and amount of your next payment. But if you choose to have your payments automatically withdrawn from your checking account, you will not receive a letter. Your bank statement is your record of payment. You can also make your payments by credit card. For details on how to pay, see your tax return instructions or visit www.irs.gov. We will also send you an annual statement showing the amount you owed at the beginning of the year, all payments made during the year, and the amount you owe at the end of the year.

If you do not make your payments on time or you have an outstanding past-due amount in a future year, you will be in default on your agreement and we may take enforcement actions, such as a Notice of Federal Tax Lien or an IRS levy, to collect the entire amount you owe. To ensure that your payments are made timely, you should consider making them by electronic funds withdrawal (see the instructions for lines 13a and 13b).

To find out more about the IRS collection process, see Pub. 594, The IRS Collection Process.

## Where To File

Attach Form 9465 to the front of your return and send it to the address shown in your tax return booklet. If you have already filed your return or you are filing this form in response to a notice, file Form 9465 by itself with the Internal Revenue Service Center at the address below for the place where you live. No street address is needed.

| IF you live in . . . | THEN use this address . . . |
|---|---|
| Alabama, Delaware, Florida, Georgia, North Carolina, Rhode Island, South Carolina, Virginia | Atlanta, GA 39901 |
| District of Columbia, Maine, Maryland, Massachusetts, New Hampshire, New York, Vermont | Andover, MA 05501 |
| New Jersey, Pennsylvania | Philadelphia, PA 19255 |
| Arkansas, Kansas, Kentucky, Louisiana, Mississippi, Oklahoma, Tennessee, Texas, West Virginia | Austin, TX 73301 |
| Alaska, Arizona, California, Colorado, Hawaii, Idaho, Montana, Nebraska, Nevada, New Mexico, Oregon, South Dakota, Utah, Washington, Wyoming | Fresno, CA 93888 |
| Connecticut, Illinois, Indiana, Iowa, Michigan, Minnesota, Missouri, North Dakota, Ohio, Wisconsin | Kansas City, MO 64999 |
| American Samoa, nonpermanent residents of Guam or the Virgin Islands*, Puerto Rico (or if excluding income under Internal Revenue Code Section 933), dual-status aliens, non-resident aliens, and anyone filing Form 4563. | Philadelphia, PA 19255 USA |
| All APO and FPO addresses, a foreign country: U.S. citizens and anyone filing Form 2555 or 2555-EZ. | Austin, TX 73301 USA |

* Permanent residents of Guam and the Virgin Islands cannot use Form 9465.

## Specific Instructions

### Line 1
If you are making this request for a joint tax return, show the names and social security numbers (SSNs) in the same order as on your tax return.

### Line 9
Enter the total amount you owe as shown on your tax return (or notice).

⚠ **CAUTION** *If the total amount you owe is more than $25,000 (including any amounts you owe from prior years), complete and attach Form 433-F, Collection Information Statement. You can get Form 433-F by visiting the IRS website at www.irs.gov.*

84     **Dealing with Debt**

## INSTALLMENT AGREEMENT REQUEST

Form 9465 (Rev. 11-2005)

### Line 10

Even if you cannot pay the full amount you owe now, you should pay as much as possible to limit penalty and interest charges. If you are filing this form with your tax return, make the payment with your return. For details on how to pay, see your tax return instructions.

If you are filing this form by itself, such as in response to a notice, attach a check or money order payable to the "United States Treasury." Do not send cash. Be sure to include:
- Your name, address, SSN, and daytime phone number.
- The tax year and tax return (for example, "2005 Form 1040") for which you are making this request.

### Line 11

You should try to make your payments large enough so that your balance due will be paid off by the due date of your next tax return.

### Line 12

You can choose the date your monthly payment is due. This can be on or after the 1st of the month, but no later than the 28th of the month. For example, if your rent or mortgage payment is due on the 1st of the month, you may want to make your installment payments on the 15th. When we approve your request, we will tell you the month and date that your first payment is due.

If we have not replied by the date you chose for your first payment, you can send the first payment to the Internal Revenue Service Center at the address shown on page 2 that applies to you. See the instructions for line 10 above to find out what to write on your payment.

### Lines 13a and 13b

**TIP** *Making your payments by electronic funds withdrawal will help ensure that your payments are made timely and that you are not in default of this agreement.*

To pay by electronic funds withdrawal from your checking account at a bank or other financial institution (such as mutual fund, brokerage firm, or credit union), fill in lines 13a and 13b. Check with your financial institution to make sure that an electronic funds withdrawal is allowed and to get the correct routing and account numbers.

**Note.** We will send you a bill for the first payment and the fee. All other payments will be electronically withdrawn.

**Line 13a.** The routing number must be nine digits. The first two digits of the routing number must be 01 through 12 or 21 through 32. Use a check to verify the routing numbers. On the sample check on this page, the routing number is 250250025. But if your check is payable through a financial institution different from the one at which you have your checking account, do not use the routing numbers on that check. Instead, contact your financial institution for the correct routing numbers.

**Line 13b.** The account number can be up to 17 characters (both numbers and letters). Include hyphens but omit spaces and special symbols. Enter the number from left to right and leave any unused boxes blank. On the sample check on this page, the account number is 20202086. Do not include the check number.

**TIP** *The electronic funds withdrawal from your checking account will not be approved unless you (and your spouse if a joint return) sign Form 9465.*

**Sample Check—Lines 13a and 13b**

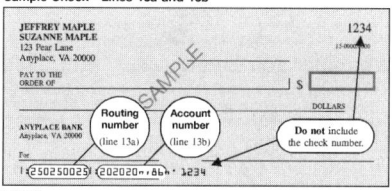

**TIP** *The routing and account numbers may be in different places on your check.*

**Privacy Act and Paperwork Reduction Act Notice.** Our legal right to ask for the information on this form is sections 6001, 6011, 6012(a), 6109, and 6159 and their regulations. We will use the information to process your request for an installment agreement. The reason we need your name and social security number is to secure proper identification. We require this information to gain access to the tax information in our files and properly respond to your request. If you do not enter the information, we may not be able to process your request.

You are not required to provide the information requested on a form that is subject to the Paperwork Reduction Act unless the form displays a valid OMB control number. Books or records relating to a form or its instructions must be retained as long as their contents may become material in the administration of any Internal Revenue law. Generally, tax returns and return information are confidential, as required by section 6103. However, we may give this information to the Department of Justice for civil and criminal litigation, and to cities, states, and the District of Columbia to carry out their tax laws. We may also disclose this information to other countries under a tax treaty, to federal and state agencies to enforce federal nontax criminal laws, or to federal law enforcement and intelligence agencies to combat terrorism.

The average time and expenses required to complete and file this form will vary depending on individual circumstances. For the estimated averages, see the instructions for your income tax return.

If you have suggestions for making this form simpler, we would be happy to hear from you. See the instructions for your income tax return.

**Dealing with Debt**

# APPENDIX 4:
# TABLE OF STATE STATUTES GOVERNING DEBT COLLECTION

| STATE | STATUTE |
| --- | --- |
| Alabama | Alabama Code §40-12-80 |
| Alaska | Alaska Statutes §§8.24.0.011 et seq. |
| Arizona | Arizona Revised Statutes Annotated §§32-1001 et seq. |
| Arkansas | Arkansas Statutes Annotated §617-21-104 et seq. |
| California | California Civil Code §§1788 et seq. |
| Colorado | Colorado Revised Statutes §§5-10101 et seq; 12-14-101 et seq. |
| Connecticut | Connecticut General Statutes Annotated §§36-243.a et seq; 42-127 et seq. |
| Delaware | Delaware Code Annotated, Title 30, §2301(13). |
| District of Columbia | D.C. Code Annotated §§22-3423 et seq; 28-3814 et seq. |
| Florida | Florida Statutes §§559.55 et seq. |
| Georgia | Georgia Code Annotated §§7-3-1 et seq. |
| Hawaii | Hawaii Revised Statutes §§443-B-1 et seq. |
| Idaho | Idaho Code §§26-2222 et seq. |
| Illinois | Illinois Annotated Statutes, Chapter 111, §§2001 et seq. |
| Indiana | Indiana Code Annotated §§25-11-1-1 et seq. |
| Iowa | Iowa Code Annotated §§537.7101 et seq. |
| Kansas | Kansas Statutes Annotated §16a-5-107. |
| Kentucky | None. |
| Louisiana | Louisiana Revised Statutes Annotated §§9:3510 et seq. |
| Maine | Maine Revised Statutes Annotated, Title 32 §§11,001 et seq; Title 9-A §§1.101 et seq. |
| Maryland | Maryland Annotated Code, Article 56 §§323 et seq; Maryland Com. Law Code Annotated, §§14-201 et seq. |
| Massachusetts | Massachusetts General Laws Annotated, Chapter 93 §§24 et seq; §49. |
| Michigan | Michigan Compiled Laws Annotated §19.655; §18.425. |
| Minnesota | None. |

**Dealing with Debt**

# TABLE OF STATE STATUTES GOVERNING DEBT COLLECTION

| STATE | STATUTE |
| --- | --- |
| Missouri | None. |
| Montana | None. |
| Nebraska | Nebraska Revised Statutes §§45-601 et seq; 45-175 et seq. |
| Nevada | Nevada Revised Statutes §§649.005 et seq. |
| New Hampshire | New Hampshire Revised Statutes Annotated §§358-C:1 et seq. |
| New Jersey | New Jersey Statutes Annotated §§45:18-1 et seq. |
| New Mexico | New Mexico Statutes Annotated §§61-18A-1 et seq. |
| New York | New York General Law §§600 et seq. |
| North Carolina | North Carolina General Statutes §§66-49.24 et seq; 75-50 et seq. |
| North Dakota | North Dakota Cent. Code §§13-05-01 et seq. |
| Ohio | None. |
| Oklahoma | None. |
| Oregon | Oregon Revised Statutes §§646.639 et seq; 697.010 et seq. |
| Pennsylvania | 18 Pennsylvania Cons. Statutes Annotated §§7311; 201-1 et seq. |
| Rhode Island | None. |
| South Carolina | South Carolina Code Annotated §37-5-108. |
| South Dakota | None. |
| Tennessee | Tennessee Code Annotated §§62-20-101 et seq. |
| Texas | Texas Revised Civ. Statutes Annotated, Arts. 5069-11.01 et seq. |
| Utah | Utah Code Annotated §§12-1-1 et seq. |
| Vermont | Vermont Statutes Annotated,, Title 9 §§2451a et seq. |
| Virginia | Virginia Code Annotated §§18.2 et seq. |
| Washington | Washington Revised Code Annotated §§19.16.100 et seq. |
| West Virginia | West Virginia Code §§47-16-1 §§18.2 et seq; 46A-2-101 et seq. |
| Wisconsin | Wisconsin Statutes Annotated §§218.04; 427.101 et seq. |
| Wyoming | Wyoming Statutes §§33-11-101 et seq. |

# APPENDIX 5: CREDITOR DEMAND LETTER

Mr. John Smith
123 Main Street
White Plains, New York

RE: Charge-A-Lot Account Number 032773

Dear Mr. Smith:

We have been retained by Charge-A-Lot, Inc. to collect the amount of Three Hundred ($300.00) Dollars which is outstanding on your account. To avoid further action, please send a check or money order for the full amount immediately.

Unless you notify us within thirty days after receipt of this letter that you dispute the validity of this debt, we will assume the debt is valid. If within that time period you notify us that you dispute the debt, or any portion of it, we will obtain verification of the debt from the creditor and send it to you, and will provide you with the name and address of the original creditor if it differs from the current creditor. This letter is an attempt to collect the debt, and any information contained will be used for that purpose.

If you would like to discuss this claim further, please contact the undersigned.

Very truly yours,

Mary Jones, Collection Supervisor
The Pay Now or Else Debt Collection Agency, Inc.

# APPENDIX 6:
# PAYMENT AGREEMENT CONFIRMATION LETTER

Mr. John Smith
123 Main Street
White Plains, New York

RE: Charge-A-Lot Account Number 032773

Dear Mr. Smith:

This letter is being sent to you to confirm your agreement to make payments on the above-referenced account so as to avoid further action being taken against you to collect this debt.

As agreed, the outstanding balance of Three Hundred ($300.00) Dollars will be paid in equal monthly installments of Fifty ($50.00) Dollars, beginning on the first of next month, for the next six months until paid in full.

If this letter accurately states the terms of our agreement, please sign where indicated below and return the letter to me in the enclosed self-addressed stamped envelope.

Very truly yours,

Mary Jones, Collection Supervisor
The Pay Now or Else Debt Collection Agency, Inc.

# APPENDIX 7:
# NOTICE TO COLLECTION AGENCY TO CEASE CONTACT

[Date]

BY CERTIFIED MAIL - RETURN RECEIPT REQUESTED

TO: [The Pay Now or Else Debt Collection Agency, Inc.]

RE: Charge-A-Lot Account Number 032773

Dear Sir/Madam:

This letter shall serve as a notice to your company to cease any further contact with me in connection with the above-referenced account. As I am sure you are aware, the law requires you to comply with this request.

I am presently unable to make payments on this account because [state reasons, e.g., illness, layoff, etc.]. I am trying to reorganize my financial situation, and intend to take care of this matter as soon as I am able. Although I have explained my circumstances to your employees, they have continued to employ collection tactics that are illegal. [Give details]. This has caused me a great amount of stress.

I would appreciate your cooperation so as to avoid having to assert my legal rights in a court of law. Thank you.

Very truly yours,

John Smith

cc: Charge-A-Lot, Inc.

cc: The Federal Trade Commission

cc: The Better Business Bureau

# APPENDIX 8:
# AGREEMENT TO COMPROMISE A DEBT

BE IT KNOWN, for good and valuable consideration, I, [Name of Creditor] ( reditor , as a creditor of [Name of Debtor] ( ebtor , hereby enter into this agreement to compromise and discharge the indebtedness due from Debtor to Creditor on the following terms and conditions:

[Specify terms and conditions, e.g.: Payment must be made within 15 days of the date of this agreement.]

The Debtor and Creditor acknowledge that the present debt due and owing Creditor is in the amount of [Dollar Amount ($xxx)] Dollars.

The parties agree that the undersigned creditor shall accept the sum of [Dollar Amount ($xxx)] Dollars as full and total payment on said debt and in complete discharge, release, satisfaction and settlement of all monies presently due, provided the sum herein shall be fully and punctually paid in the following manner: [Specify manner of payment, e.g., by certified check or money order, etc.].

In the event the Debtor fails to fully and punctually pay the compromised amount, Creditor shall have full rights to prosecute Creditor claim for the full amount of [Dollar Amount ($xxx)] Dollars, less credits for payments made.

In the event of default in payment the Debtor agrees to pay all reasonable attorneys fees and costs of collection.

This agreement shall be binding upon and inure to the benefit of the parties, their successors, assigns and personal representatives.

DATED:                         DATED:
BY: _____    BY: _____
[SIGNATURE LINE—DEBTOR]      [SIGNATURE LINE—CREDITOR]

# APPENDIX 9:
# FTC CONSUMER COMPLAINT FORM

## FTC CONSUMER COMPLAINT FORM

Use this form to submit a complaint to the Federal Trade Commission (FTC) Bureau of Consumer Protection about a particular company or organization. This form also may be used to submit a complaint to the FTC concerning media violence. The information you provide is up to you. However, if you do not provide your name or other information, it may be impossible for us to refer, respond to, or investigate your complaint or request. To learn how we use the information you provide, please read our Privacy Policy.

While the FTC does not resolve individual consumer problems, your complaint helps us investigate fraud, and can lead to law enforcement action. The FTC enters Internet, telemarketing, identity theft and other fraud-related complaints into Consumer Sentinel®, a secure, online database available to hundreds of civil and criminal law enforcement agencies worldwide.

We use secure socket layer (SSL) encryption to protect the transmission of the information you submit to us when you use our secure online forms. The information you provide to us is stored securely.

**IMPORTANT:**

* If you want to file a complaint about a violation of National Do Not Call Registry or register your telephone number on the Registry, Please go to www.donotcall.gov

* If you want to file a report about Identity Theft, please use our Identity Theft Complaint Form.

* If you want to file a complaint about an online transaction that involves a foreign company, please use our econsumer.gov complaint form.

If you have a specific complaint about unsolicited commercial e-mail (spam), use the form below. You can forward spam directly to the Commission at SPAM@UCE.GOV without using the complaint form.

FTC CONSUMER COMPLAINT FORM

## How Do We Reach You?

First Name:

Last Name:

Age Range (check one):
___ 12 and Under
___ 13-17
___ 18-19
___ 20-29
___ 30-39
___ 40-49
___ 50-59
___ 60-64
___ 65-69
___ 70-79
___ 80 and Over

Street Address:

City:

State:

Country:

Zip Code:

E-Mail Address:

Home Phone:

Work Phone:

Social Security Number (Enter Only For Complaints Relating to the Accuracy of Your Credit Report):

**FTC CONSUMER COMPLAINT FORM**

## Tell Us Your Complaint…

Subject of Your Complaint (check one):
- ___ Apparel/Accessories
- ___ Automobiles
- ___ Business Opportunities, Multi-Level Marketing, Education
- ___ Children's Advertising
- ___ Computers/Internet Servicing
- ___ Consumer Leasing
- ___ Credit Discrimination
- ___ Credit Reports
- ___ Debt Collection
- ___ Direct Marketing-Telemarketing/Mail Order
- ___ Electric Funds Transfer
- ___ Food Beverages
- ___ Health
- ___ Home
- ___ Investment
- ___ Lending
- ___ Media Violence
- ___ Privacy
- ___ Professional Services
- ___ Telephone, Cell Phone and VOIP Services
- ___ Work Education

Name of Company You Are Complaining About:

Check if Company Name Is Unknown: ___

Name of Product You Are Complaining About:

Street Address:

City:

State:

Country:

# FTC CONSUMER COMPLAINT FORM

Zip Code:

Company Website:

Company E-Mail Address:

Phone Number:

How Did the Company Initially Contact You?
___ E-mail
___ Fax
___ In Person
___ Internet (Other)
___ Internet Website
___ Mail
___ Phone
___ Print
___ TV/Radio
___ Unknown
___ Wireless

How Much Did the Company Ask You to Pay?

How Much Did You Actually Pay the Company?

How Did You Pay the Company?
___ American Express Credit Report
___ Bank Account Debit
___ Cash
___ Cash Advance
___ Cashier's Check
___ Certified Check
___ Discover Credit Card
___ MasterCard Credit Card
___ Not Reported
___ Other Credit Card
___ Other Type of Money Order
___ Payroll Allotment
___ Personal Check
___ Postal Money Order

# FTC CONSUMER COMPLAINT FORM

___ Telephone Bill
___ Unknown
___ Visa Credit Card
___ Wire Transfer

Did You File a Dispute with the Credit Bureau?
___ Yes
___ No

Did You File a Dispute with the Credit Bureau More Than 45 Days Ago?
___ Yes
___ No
___ Do Not Know

**REPRESENTATIVE OR SALESPERSON**

First Name:

Last Name:

Date Company Contacted You:

Explain Your Problem: (Please limit your complaint to 2000 characters):

# APPENDIX 10: CREDIT CARD ISSUER ITEM DISPUTE LETTER

[Name of Credit Card Issuer]
[Address]
[City, State, Zip Code]

Attn: Billing Inquiries

I am writing to dispute a billing error in the amount of $_____ on my account. The amount is inaccurate because (describe the problem). I am requesting that the error be corrected, that any finance and other charges related to the disputed amount be credited as well, and that I receive an accurate statement.

Enclosed are copies of (use this sentence to describe any enclosed information, such as sales slips, payment records) supporting my position. Please investigate this matter and correct the billing error as soon as possible.

Sincerely,

John Doe

Enclosures: (List what you are enclosing.)

# APPENDIX 11:
# FAIR DEBT COLLECTION PRACTICES ACT

**TITLE 15 § 1692. CONGRESSIONAL FINDINGS AND DECLARATION OF PURPOSE**

(a) Abusive practices.

There is abundant evidence of the use of abusive, deceptive, and unfair debt collection practices by many debt collectors. Abusive debt collection practices contribute to the number of personal bankruptcies, to marital instability, to the loss of jobs, and to invasions of individual privacy.

(b) Inadequacy of laws.

Existing laws and procedures for redressing these injuries are inadequate to protect consumers.

(c) Available non-abusive collection methods.

Means other than misrepresentation or other abusive debt collection practices are available for the effective collection of debts.

(d) Interstate commerce.

Abusive debt collection practices are carried on to a substantial extent in interstate commerce and through means and instrumentalities of such commerce. Even where abusive debt collection practices are purely intrastate in character, they nevertheless directly affect interstate commerce.

(e) Purposes.

It is the purpose of this subchapter to eliminate abusive debt collection practices by debt collectors, to insure that those debt collectors who refrain from using abusive debt collection practices are not competitively disadvantaged, and to promote consistent State action to protect consumers against debt collection abuses.

# FAIR DEBT COLLECTION PRACTICES ACT

## SECTION 1692A. DEFINITIONS

As used in this subchapter:

(1) The term "Commission" means the Federal Trade Commission.

(2) The term "communication" means the conveying of information regarding a debt directly or indirectly to any person through any medium.

(3) The term "consumer" means any natural person obligated or allegedly obligated to pay any debt.

(4) The term "creditor" means any person who offers or extends credit creating a debt or to whom a debt is owed, but such term does not include any person to the extent that he receives an assignment or transfer of a debt in default solely for the purpose of facilitating collection of such debt for another.

(5) The term "debt" means any obligation or alleged obligation of a consumer to pay money arising out of a transaction in which the money, property, insurance, or services which are the subject of the transaction are primarily for personal, family, or household purposes, whether or not such obligation has been reduced to judgment.

(6) The term "debt collector" means any person who uses any instrumentality of interstate commerce or the mails in any business the principal purpose of which is the collection of any debts, or who regularly collects or attempts to collect, directly or indirectly, debts owed or due or asserted to be owed or due another. Notwithstanding the exclusion provided by clause (F) of the last sentence of this paragraph, the term includes any creditor who, in the process of collecting his own debts, uses any name other than his own which would indicate that a third person is collecting or attempting to collect such debts. For the purpose of section 1692f (6)] of this title, such term also includes any person who uses any instrumentality of interstate commerce or the mails in any business the principal purpose of which is the enforcement of security interests. The term does not include:

(A) any officer or employee of a creditor while, in the name of the creditor, collecting debts for such creditor;

(B) any person while acting as a debt collector for another person, both of whom are related by common ownership or affiliated by corporate control, if the person acting as a debt collector does so only for persons to whom it is so related or affiliated and if the principal business of such person is not the collection of debts;

(C) any officer or employee of the United States or any State to the extent that collecting or attempting to collect any debt is in the performance of his official duties;

(D) any person while serving or attempting to serve legal process on any other person in connection with the judicial enforcement of any debt;

(E) any nonprofit organization which, at the request of consumers, performs bona fide consumer credit counseling and assists consumers in the liquidation of their debts by receiving payments from such consumers and distributing such amounts to creditors; and

(F) any person collecting or attempting to collect any debt owed or due or asserted to be owed or due another to the extent such activity (i) is incidental to a bona fide fiduciary obligation or a bona fide escrow arrangement; (ii) concerns a debt which was originated by such person; (iii) concerns a debt which was not in default at the time it was obtained by such person; or (iv) concerns a debt obtained by such person as a secured party in a commercial credit transaction involving the creditor.

(7) The term "location information" means a consumer's place of abode and his telephone number at such place, or his place of employment.

(8) The term "State" means any State, territory, or possession of the United States, the District of Columbia, the Commonwealth of Puerto Rico, or any political subdivision of any of the foregoing.

## SECTION 1692B. ACQUISITION OF LOCATION INFORMATION.

Any debt collector communicating with any person other than the consumer for the purpose of acquiring location information about the consumer shall:

(1) identify himself, state that he is confirming or correcting location information concerning the consumer, and, only if expressly requested, identify his employer;

(2) not state that such consumer owes any debt;

(3) not communicate with any such person more than once unless requested to do so by such person or unless the debt collector reasonably believes that the earlier response of such person is erroneous or incomplete and that such person now has correct or complete location information;

(4) not communicate by postcard;

(5) not use any language or symbol on any envelope or in the contents of any communication effected by the mails or telegram that indicates that the debt collector is in the debt collection business or that the communication relates to the collection of a debt; and

(6) after the debt collector knows the consumer is represented by an attorney with regard to the subject debt and has knowledge of, or can readily ascertain, such attorney's name and address, not communicate with any person other than that attorney, unless the attorney fails to respond within a reasonable period of time to communication from the debt collector.

### SECTION 1692C. COMMUNICATION IN CONNECTION WITH DEBT COLLECTION

(a) Communication with the consumer generally.

Without the prior consent of the consumer given directly to the debt collector or the express permission of a court of competent jurisdiction, a debt collector may not communicate with a consumer in connection with the collection of any debt:

(1) at any unusual time or place or a time or place known or which should be known to be inconvenient to the consumer. In the absence of knowledge of circumstances to the contrary, a debt collector shall assume that the convenient time for communicating with a consumer is after 8 o'clock antimeridian and before 9 o'clock postmeridian, local time at the consumer's location;

(2) if the debt collector knows the consumer is represented by an attorney with respect to such debt and has knowledge of, or can readily ascertain, such attorney's name and address, unless the attorney fails to respond within a reasonable period of time to a communication from the debt collector or unless the attorney consents to direct communication with the consumer; or

(3) at the consumer's place of employment if the debt collector knows or has reason to know that the consumer's employer prohibits the consumer from receiving such communication.

(b) Communication with third parties.

Except as provided in section §1692b of this title, without the prior consent of the consumer given directly to the debt collector, or the express permission of a court of competent jurisdiction, or as reasonably necessary to effectuate a postjudgment judicial remedy, a debt collector may not communicate, in connection with the collection of any debt, with any person other than the consumer, his attorney, a consumer reporting agency if otherwise permitted by law, the creditor, the attorney of the creditor, or the attorney of the debt collector.

(c) Ceasing communication.

If a consumer notifies a debt collector in writing that the consumer refuses to pay a debt or that the consumer wishes the debt collector to cease further communication with the consumer, the debt collector shall not communicate further with the consumer with respect to such debt, except:

(1) to advise the consumer that the debt collector's further efforts are being terminated;

(2) to notify the consumer that the debt collector or creditor may invoke specified remedies which are ordinarily invoked by such debt collector or creditor; or

(3) where applicable, to notify the consumer that the debt collector or creditor intends to invoke a specified remedy. If such notice from the consumer is made by mail, notification shall be complete upon receipt.

(d) "Consumer" defined.

For the purpose of this section, the term "consumer" includes the consumer's spouse, parent (if the consumer is a minor), guardian, executor, or administrator.

## SECTION 1692D. HARASSMENT OR ABUSE

A debt collector may not engage in any conduct the natural consequence of which is to harass, oppress, or abuse any person in connection with the collection of a debt. Without limiting the general application of the foregoing, the following conduct is a violation of this section:

(1) The use or threat of use of violence or other criminal means to harm the physical person, reputation, or property of any person.

(2) The use of obscene or profane language or language the natural consequence of which is to abuse the hearer or reader.

(3) The publication of a list of consumers who allegedly refuse to pay debts, except to a consumer reporting agency or to persons meeting the requirements of section 1681a (f) or 1681b (3) of this title.

(4) The advertisement for sale of any debt to coerce payment of the debt.

(5) Causing a telephone to ring or engaging any person in telephone conversation repeatedly or continuously with intent to annoy, abuse or harass any person at the called number.

# FAIR DEBT COLLECTION PRACTICES ACT

(6) Except as provided in section 1692b of this title, the placement of telephone calls without meaningful disclosure of the caller's identity.

## SECTION 1692E. FALSE OR MISLEADING REPRESENTATIONS

A debt collector may not use any false, deceptive, or misleading representation or means in connection with the collection of any debt. Without limiting the general application of the foregoing, the following conduct is a violation of this section:

(1) The false representation or implication that the debt collector is vouched for, bonded by, or affiliated with the United States or any State, including the use of any badge, uniform, or facsimile thereof.

(2) The false representation of:

(A) the character, amount, or legal status of any debt; or

(B) any services rendered or compensation which may be lawfully received by any debt collector for the collection of a debt.

(3) The false representation or implication that any individual is an attorney or that any communication is from an attorney.

(4) The representation or implication that nonpayment of any debt will result in the arrest or imprisonment of any person or the seizure, garnishment, attachment, or sale of any property or wages of any person unless such action is lawful and the debt collector or creditor intends to take such action.

(5) The threat to take any action that cannot legally be taken or that is not intended to be taken.

(6) The false representation or implication that a sale, referral, or other transfer of any interest in a debt shall cause the consumer to:

(A) lose any claim or defense to payment of the debt; or

(B) become subject to any practice prohibited by this subchapter.

(7) The false representation or implication that the consumer committed any crime or other conduct in order to disgrace the consumer.

(8) Communicating or threatening to communicate to any person credit information which is known or which should be known to be false, including the failure to communicate that a disputed debt is disputed.

(9) The use or distribution of any written communication which simulates or is falsely represented to be a document authorized, issued, or approved by any court, official, or agency of the United States or

any State, or which creates a false impression as to its source, authorization, or approval.

(10) The use of any false representation or deceptive means to collect or attempt to collect any debt or to obtain information concerning a consumer.

(11) The failure to disclose in the initial written communication with the consumer and, in addition, if the initial communication with the is oral, in that initial oral communication, that the debt collector is attempting to collect a debt and that any information obtained will be used for that purpose, and the failure to disclose in subsequent communications that the communication is from a debt collector, except that this paragraph shall not apply to a formal pleading made in connection with a legal action.

(12) The false representation or implication that accounts have been turned over to innocent purchasers for value.

(13) The false representation or implication that documents are legal process.

(14) The use of any business, company, or organization name other than the true name of the debt collector's business, company, or organization.

(15) The false representation or implication that documents are not legal process forms or do not require action by the consumer.

(16) The false representation or implication that a debt collector operates or is employed by a consumer reporting agency as defined by section 1681a (f)] of this title.

## SECTION 1692F. UNFAIR PRACTICES

A debt collector may not use unfair or unconscionable means to collect or attempt to collect any debt. Without limiting the general application of the foregoing, the following conduct is a violation of this section:

(1) The collection of any amount (including any interest, fee, charge, or expense incidental to the principal obligation) unless such amount is expressly authorized by the agreement creating the debt or permitted by law.

(2) The acceptance by a debt collector from any person of a check or other payment instrument postdated by more than five days unless such person is notified in writing of the debt collector's intent to deposit such check or instrument not more than ten nor less than three business days prior to such deposit.

**FAIR DEBT COLLECTION PRACTICES ACT**

(3) The solicitation by a debt collector of any postdated check or other postdated payment instrument for the purpose of threatening or instituting criminal prosecution.

(4) Depositing or threatening to deposit any postdated check or other postdated payment instrument prior to the date on such check or instrument.

(5) Causing charges to be made to any person for communications by concealment of the true purpose of the communication. Such charges include, but are not limited to, collect telephone calls and telegram fees.

(6) Taking or threatening to take any nonjudicial action to effect dispossession or disablement of property if:

(A) there is no present right to possession of the property claimed as collateral through an enforceable security interest;

(B) there is no present intention to take possession of the property; or

(C) the property is exempt by law from such dispossession or disablement.

(7) Communicating with a consumer regarding a debt by postcard.

(8) Using any language or symbol, other than the debt collector's address, on any envelope when communicating with a consumer by use of the mails or by telegram, except that a debt collector may use his business name if such name does not indicate that he is in the debt collection business.

### SECTION 1692G. VALIDATION OF DEBTS

(a) Notice of debt; contents.

Within five days after the initial communication with a consumer in connection with the collection of any debt, a debt collector shall, unless the following information is contained in the initial communication or the consumer has paid the debt, send the consumer a written notice containing:

(1) the amount of the debt;

(2) the name of the creditor to whom the debt is owed;

(3) a statement that unless the consumer, within thirty days after receipt of the notice, disputes the validity of the debt, or any portion thereof, the debt will be assumed to be valid by the debt collector;

(4) a statement that if the consumer notifies the debt collector in writing within the thirty-day period that the debt, or any portion thereof, is disputed, the debt collector will obtain verification of the debt or a copy of a judgment against the consumer and a copy of such verification or judgment will be mailed to the consumer by the debt collector; and

(5) a statement that, upon the consumer's written request within the thirty-day period, the debt collector will provide the consumer with the name and address of the original creditor, if different from the current creditor.

(b) Disputed debts.

If the consumer notifies the debt collector in writing within the thirty-day period described in subsection (a) that the debt, or any portion thereof, is disputed, or that the consumer requests the name and address of the original creditor, the debt collector shall cease collection of the debt, or any disputed portion thereof, until the debt collector obtains verification of the debt or a copy of a judgment, or the name and address of the original creditor, and a copy of such verification or judgment, or name and address of the original creditor, is mailed to the consumer by the debt collector.

(c) Admission of liability.

The failure of a consumer to dispute the validity of a debt under this section may not be construed by any court as an admission of liability by the consumer.

## SECTION 1692H. MULTIPLE DEBTS

If any consumer owes multiple debts and makes any single payment to any debt collector with respect to such debts, such debt collector may not apply such payment to any debt which is disputed by the consumer and, where applicable, shall apply such payment in accordance with the consumer's directions.

## SECTION 1692I. LEGAL ACTIONS BY DEBT COLLECTORS

(a) Venue.

Any debt collector who brings any legal action on a debt against any consumer shall:

(1) in the case of an action to enforce an interest in real property securing the consumer's obligation, bring such action only in a judicial district or similar legal entity in which such real property is located; or

(2) in the case of an action not described in paragraph (1), bring such action only in the judicial district or similar legal entity:

(A) in which such consumer signed the contract sued upon; or

(B) in which such consumer resides at the commencement of the action.

(b) Authorization of actions.

Nothing in this subchapter shall be construed to authorize the bringing of legal actions by debt collectors.

## SECTION 1692J. FURNISHING CERTAIN DECEPTIVE FORMS

(a) It is unlawful to design, compile, and furnish any form knowing that such form would be used to create the false belief in a consumer that a person other than the creditor of such consumer is participating in the collection of or in an attempt to collect a debt such consumer allegedly owes such creditor, when in fact such person is not so participating.

(b) Any person who violates this section shall be liable to the same extent and in the same manner as a debt collector is liable under section 1692k of this title for failure to comply with a provision of this subchapter.

## SECTION 1692K. CIVIL LIABILITY

(a) Amount of damages.

Except as otherwise provided by this section, any debt collector who fails to comply with any provision of this subchapter with respect to any person is liable to such person in an amount equal to the sum of:

(1) any actual damage sustained by such person as a result of such failure;

(2)(A) in the case of any action by an individual, such additional damages as the court may allow, but not exceeding $1,000; or

(2)(B) in the case of a class action, (i) such amount for each named plaintiff as could be recovered under subparagraph (A), and (ii) such amount as the court may allow for all other class members, without regard to a minimum individual recovery, not to exceed the lesser of $500,000 or 1 per centum of the net worth of the debt collector; and

(3) in the case of any successful action to enforce the foregoing liability, the costs of the action, together with a reasonable attorney's fee as determined by the court. On a finding by the court that an action under this section was brought in bad faith and for the purpose of ha-

rassment, the court may award to defendant attorney's fees reasonable in relation to the work expended and costs.

(b) Factors considered by court.

In determining the amount of liability in any action under subsection (a), the court shall consider, among other relevant factors:

(1) in any individual action under subsection (a)(2)(A), the frequency and persistence of noncompliance by the debt collector, the nature of such noncompliance, and the extent to which such noncompliance was intentional; or

(2) in any class action under subsection (a)(2)(B), the frequency and persistence of noncompliance by the debt collector, the nature of such noncompliance, the resources of the debt collector, the number of persons adversely affected, and the extent to which the debt collector's noncompliance was intentional.

(c) Intent.

A debt collector may not be held liable in any action brought under this title if the debt collector shows by a preponderance of evidence that the violation was not intentional and resulted from a bona fide error the maintenance of procedures reasonably adapted to avoid any such error.

(d) Jurisdiction.

An action to enforce any liability created by this subchapter may be brought in any appropriate United States district court without regard to the amount in controversy, or in any other court of competent jurisdiction, within one year from the date on which the violation occurs.

(e) Advisory opinions of Commission.

No provision of this section imposing any liability shall apply to any act done or omitted in good faith in conformity with any advisory opinion of the Commission, notwithstanding that after such act or omission has occurred, such opinion is amended, rescinded, or determined by judicial or other authority to be invalid for any reason.

## SECTION 1692L. ADMINISTRATIVE ENFORCEMENT

(a) Federal Trade Commission.

Compliance with this subchapter shall be enforced by the Commission, except to the extent that enforcement of the requirements imposed under this title is specifically committed to another agency under subsection (b) of this section. For purpose of the exercise by the Commission of its functions and powers under the Federal Trade Commission Act [15 U.S.C. 41 et seq.], a violation of this subchapter shall be deemed an unfair or deceptive act or practice in violation of that Act. All of the functions and powers of the Commission under the Federal Trade Commission Act are available to the Commission to enforce compliance by any person with this subchapter, irrespective of whether that person is engaged in commerce or meets any other jurisdictional tests in the Federal Trade Commission Act, including the power to enforce the provisions of this subchapter in the same manner as if the violation had been a violation of a Federal Trade Commission trade regulation rule.

(b) Applicable provisions of law.

Compliance with any requirements imposed under this subchapter shall be enforced under:

(1) section 8 of the Federal Deposit Insurance Act [12 U.S.C. 1818], in the case of:

(A) national banks, and Federal branches and Federal agencies of foreign banks, by the Office of the Comptroller of the Currency;

(B) member banks of the Federal Reserve System (other than national banks), branches and agencies of foreign banks (other than Federal branches, Federal agencies, and insured State branches of foreign banks), commercial lending companies owned or controlled by foreign banks, and organizations operating under section 25 or 25(a) of the Federal Reserve Act [12 U.S.C. 601 et seq., 611 et seq.], by the Board of Governors of the Federal Reserve System; and

(C) banks insured by the Federal Deposit Insurance Corporation (other than members of the Federal Reserve System) and insured State branches of foreign banks, by the Board of Directors of the Federal Deposit Insurance Corporation;

(2) section 8 of the Federal Deposit Insurance Act [12 U.S.C. 1818], by the Director of the Office of Thrift Supervision, in the case of a savings association the deposits of which are insured by the Federal Deposit Insurance Corporation;

(3) the Federal Credit Union Act [12 U.S.C. 1751 et seq.] by the National Credit Union Administration Board with respect to any Federal credit union;

(4) subtitle IV of title 49, by the Secretary of Transportation, with respect to all carriers subject to the jurisdiction of the Surface Transportation Board;

(5) part A of Subtitle VII of title 49, by the Secretary of Transportation with respect to any air carrier or any foreign air carrier subject to that part; and

(6) the Packers and Stockyards Act, 1921 [7 U.S.C. 181 et Seq.], (except as provided in section 406 of that Act [7 U.S.C. 226, 227]), by the Secretary of Agriculture with respect to any activities subject to that Act.

The terms used in paragraph (1) that are not defined in this subchapter or otherwise defined in section 3(s) of the Federal Deposit Insurance Act (12 U.S.C. 1813 (s)) shall have the meaning given to them in section 1(b) of the International Banking Act of 1978 (12 U.S.C. 3101).

(c) Agency powers.

For the purpose of the exercise by any agency referred to in subsection (b) of its powers under any Act referred to in that subsection, a violation of any requirement imposed under this subchapter shall be deemed to be a violation of a requirement imposed under that Act. In addition to its powers under any provision of law specifically referred to in subsection (b), each of the agencies referred to in that subsection may exercise, for the purpose of enforcing compliance with any requirement imposed under this subchapter any other authority conferred on it by law, except as provided in subsection (d) of this section.

(d) Rules and regulations.

Neither the Commission nor any other agency referred to in subsection (b) may promulgate trade regulation rules or other regulations with respect to the collection of debts by debt collectors as defined in this subchapter.

## SECTION 1692M. REPORTS TO CONGRESS BY THE COMMISSION; VIEWS OF OTHER FEDERAL AGENCIES

(a) Not later than one year after the effective date of this subchapter and at one-year intervals thereafter, the Commission shall make reports to the Congress concerning the administration of its functions under this subchapter, including such recommendations as the Commission deems necessary or appropriate. In addition, each report of the Commission shall include its assessment of the extent to which compliance with this subchapter is being achieved and a summary of the enforcement actions taken by the Commission under section 1692l of this title.

(b) In the exercise of its functions under this subchapter, the Commission may obtain upon request the views of any other Federal agency which exercises enforcement functions under section 1692l of this title.

### SECTION 1692N. RELATION TO STATE LAWS

This subchapter does not annul, alter, or affect, or exempt any person subject to the provisions of this subchapter from complying with the laws of any State with respect to debt collection practices, except to the extent that those laws are inconsistent with any provision of this subchapter, and then only to the extent of the inconsistency. For purposes of this section, a State law is not inconsistent with this subchapter if the protection such law affords any consumer is greater than the protection provided by this subchapter.

### SECTION 1692O. EXEMPTION FOR STATE REGULATION

The Commission shall by regulation exempt from the requirements of this subchapter any class of debt collection practices within any State if the Commission determines that under the law of that State that class of debt collection practices is subject to requirements substantially similar to those imposed by this subchapter, and that there is adequate provision for enforcement.

# APPENDIX 12: DEBT COLLECTION HARASSMENT COMPLAINT

[CAPTION]

**COMPLAINT**

**I. INTRODUCTION**

This is an action brought by an individual consumer for statutory damages under the Fair Debt Collection Practices Act, 15 U.S.C. Section 1692 et. seq. (hereinafter referred to as the "FDCPA"), resulting from Defendants' violations of the statute by engaging in abusive, deceptive and unfair debt collection practices.

**II. JURISDICTION**

The jurisdiction of this court to determine this action arises under 15 U.S.C. Section 1692k(d) and 28 U.S.C. Section 1337.

**III. PARTIES**

The plaintiff, John Smith, is a natural person residing at 123 Main Street, City of White Plains, County of Westchester, State of New York.

The defendant, The Pay Now or Else Debt Collection Agency, Inc. is a corporation with its principal place of business located at 1 Park Avenue, New York, New York. The defendant is engaged in the business of collecting debts on behalf of third parties.

### IV. STATEMENT OF FACTS

On or about January 1, 2006, defendant telephoned plaintiff at his place of employment, demanding payment of a debt allegedly due a creditor, Charge-A-Lot, Inc., under Account Number 032773.

The plaintiff advised the defendant that he could not receive telephone calls at his place of employment. Nevertheless, the defendant telephoned the plaintiff three additional times on that same day.

Plaintiff thereafter sent a letter to defendant advising them that he did not want to be contacted concerning collection of this debt, either by telephone or in writing. This letter was sent by certified mail with a return receipt requested.

A copy of plaintiff's letter dated January 3, 2006 is attached as Exhibit A. A copy of the return receipt card signed by a representative of defendant on January 5, 2006 is attached as Exhibit B.

On February 1, 2006, defendant telephoned plaintiff at his home and spoke with his minor child. Defendant used threatening and abusive language to the child, to wit: the defendant stated that the child's father would be sent to jail if he did not pay his bills.

On February 3, 2006, defendant again telephoned plaintiff's place of employment. Plaintiff was not present at the time. Plaintiff's co-worker, Mary Jones, received the telephone call. Defendant conduct was abusive and threatening, as set forth in the affidavit of Mary Jones, attached as Exhibit C.

Defendant's violations of the statute include, but are not limited to the following:

[Specify statutory violations]

As a result of the defendant's violations of the FDCPA, plaintiff has suffered actual damages, including mental distress and medical expenses, and is entitled to an award of statutory damages, legal fees and costs.

WHEREFORE, plaintiff respectfully requests that judgment be entered against defendant as follows:

1. Actual damages;

2. Statutory damages in the amount of One Thousand ($1,000) Dollars per violation as set forth in 15 U.S.C. Section 1692k;

Legal fees and costs as set forth in 15 U.S.C. Section 1692k;

Any additional relief as to this Court appears just and reasonable.

Plaintiff requests a jury trial.

**DEBT COLLECTION HARASSMENT COMPLAINT**

[Date]

By: _____

[Attorney Name/Address/Telephone]

[Verification by plaintiff]

# APPENDIX 13:
# SATISFACTION OF JUDGMENT AND RELEASE OF LIEN

BE IT KNOWN, that [Name of Beholder] ("Lienholder"), of [Address], contracted with [Name of Contracting Party] on [Date of Contract], to furnish labor and/or materials for construction on the premises owned by [Name of Property Owner], located at [Address].

On [Date of Filing], the lienholder filed a notice of lien against the above property in the Office of the County Clerk, County of _____, in the State of _____. Said lien was duly recorded in [Set forth recording information] of the Lien Records of the County.

In consideration of [Dollar Amount ($xxx)] Dollars, receipt of which is acknowledged, lienholder releases the above described property and the owner personally from all liability arising from the labor performed and/or materials furnished by lienholder under the terms of the above-mentioned contract, and authorizes and directs that the above-mentioned lien be discharged of record.

DATED:

BY: _____

[SIGNATURE LINE—LIENHOLDER]

STATE OF

COUNTY OF

On the ___ day of _____, 20___, before me personally came [Name of Lienholder], to me known to be the individual described in and who executed the foregoing instrument, and acknowledged that he/she executed the same.

_____

[NOTARY PUBLIC]

# APPENDIX 14: DEBTOR'S VOLUNTARY BANKRUPTCY PETITION (OFFICIAL FORM 1)

*(Official Form 1) (10/05)*

| United States Bankruptcy Court<br>District of _____ | Voluntary Petition |
|---|---|

| Name of Debtor (if individual, enter Last, First, Middle): | Name of Joint Debtor (Spouse) (Last, First, Middle): |
|---|---|
| All Other Names used by the Debtor in the last 8 years (include married, maiden, and trade names): | All Other Names used by the Joint Debtor in the last 8 years (include married, maiden, and trade names): |
| Last four digits of Soc. Sec./Complete EIN or other Tax I.D. No. (if more than one, state all): | Last four digits of Soc. Sec./Complete EIN or other Tax I.D. No. (if more than one, state all): |
| Street Address of Debtor (No. & Street, City, and State):<br>ZIPCODE | Street Address of Joint Debtor (No. & Street, City, and State):<br>ZIPCODE |
| County of Residence or of the Principal Place of Business: | County of Residence or of the Principal Place of Business: |
| Mailing Address of Debtor (if different from street address):<br>ZIPCODE | Mailing Address of Joint Debtor (if different from street address):<br>ZIPCODE |
| Location of Principal Assets of Business Debtor (if different from street address above):<br>ZIPCODE | |

**Type of Debtor** (Form of Organization) (Check **one** box.)
- ☐ Individual (includes Joint Debtors)
- ☐ Corporation (includes LLC and LLP)
- ☐ Partnership
- ☐ Other (If debtor is not one of the above entities, check this box and provide the information requested below.)

State type of entity: _____

**Nature of Business** (Check all applicable boxes.)
- ☐ Health Care Business
- ☐ Single Asset Real Estate as defined in 11 U.S.C. § 101 (51B)
- ☐ Railroad
- ☐ Stockbroker
- ☐ Commodity Broker
- ☐ Clearing Bank
- ☐ Nonprofit Organization qualified under 26 U.S.C. § 501(c)(3)

**Chapter of Bankruptcy Code Under Which the Petition is Filed** (Check one box)
- ☐ Chapter 7
- ☐ Chapter 11
- ☐ Chapter 9
- ☐ Chapter 12
- ☐ Chapter 13
- ☐ Chapter 15 Petition for Recognition of a Foreign Main Proceeding
- ☐ Chapter 15 Petition for Recognition of a Foreign Nonmain Proceeding

**Nature of Debts** (Check one box)
- ☐ Consumer/Non-Business
- ☐ Business

**Chapter 11 Debtors**
Check one box:
- ☐ Debtor is a small business debtor as defined in 11 U.S.C. § 101(51D).
- ☐ Debtor is not a small business debtor as defined in 11 U.S.C. § 101(51D).

Check if:
- ☐ Debtor's aggregate noncontingent liquidated debts owed to non-insiders or affiliates are less than $2 million.

**Filing Fee** (Check one box)
- ☐ Full Filing Fee attached
- ☐ Filing Fee to be paid in installments (Applicable to individuals only). Must attach signed application for the court's consideration certifying that the debtor is unable to pay fee except in installments. Rule 1006(b). See Official Form 3A.
- ☐ Filing Fee waiver requested (Applicable to chapter 7 individuals only). Must attach signed application for the court's consideration. See Official Form 3B.

THIS SPACE IS FOR COURT USE ONLY

**Statistical/Administrative Information**
- ☐ Debtor estimates that funds will be available for distribution to unsecured creditors.
- ☐ Debtor estimates that, after any exempt property is excluded and administrative expenses paid, there will be no funds available for distribution to unsecured creditors.

Estimated Number of Creditors:
| 1-49 | 50-99 | 100-199 | 200-999 | 1,000-5,000 | 5,001-10,000 | 10,001-25,000 | 25,001-50,000 | 50,001-100,000 | OVER 100,000 |
|---|---|---|---|---|---|---|---|---|---|
| ☐ | ☐ | ☐ | ☐ | ☐ | ☐ | ☐ | ☐ | ☐ | ☐ |

Estimated Assets:
| $0 to $50,000 | $50,001 to $100,000 | $100,001 to $500,000 | $500,001 to $1 million | $1,000,001 to $10 million | $10,000,001 to $50 million | $50,000,001 to $100 million | More than $100 million |
|---|---|---|---|---|---|---|---|
| ☐ | ☐ | ☐ | ☐ | ☐ | ☐ | ☐ | ☐ |

Estimated Debts:
| $0 to $50,000 | $50,001 to $100,000 | $100,001 to $500,000 | $500,001 to $1 million | $1,000,001 to $10 million | $10,000,001 to $50 million | $50,000,001 to $100 million | More than $100 million |
|---|---|---|---|---|---|---|---|
| ☐ | ☐ | ☐ | ☐ | ☐ | ☐ | ☐ | ☐ |

## DEBTOR'S VOLUNTARY BANKRUPTCY PETITION (OFFICIAL FORM 1)

(Official Form 1) (10/05)

FORM B1, Page 2

| Voluntary Petition<br>*(This page must be completed and filed in every case)* | Name of Debtor(s): | |
|---|---|---|
| **Prior Bankruptcy Case Filed Within Last 8 Years** (If more than one, attach additional sheet) | | |
| Location<br>Where Filed: | Case Number: | Date Filed: |
| **Pending Bankruptcy Case Filed by any Spouse, Partner or Affiliate of this Debtor** (If more than one, attach additional sheet) | | |
| Name of Debtor: | Case Number: | Date Filed: |
| District: | Relationship: | Judge: |

| Exhibit A | Exhibit B |
|---|---|
| (To be completed if debtor is required to file periodic reports (e.g., forms 10K and 10Q) with the Securities and Exchange Commission pursuant to Section 13 or 15(d) of the Securities Exchange Act of 1934 and is requesting relief under chapter 11.) | (To be completed if debtor is an individual whose debts are primarily consumer debts.)<br>I, the attorney for the petitioner named in the foregoing petition, declare that I have informed the petitioner that [he or she] may proceed under chapter 7, 11, 12, or 13 of title 11, United States Code, and have explained the relief available under each such chapter. I further certify that I delivered to the debtor the notice required by § 342(b) of the Bankruptcy Code. |
| ☐ Exhibit A is attached and made a part of this petition. | X _____<br>Signature of Attorney for Debtor(s)   Date |

| Exhibit C | Certification Concerning Debt Counseling<br>by Individual/Joint Debtor(s) |
|---|---|
| Does the debtor own or have possession of any property that poses or is alleged to pose a threat of imminent and identifiable harm to public health or safety? | ☐ I/we have received approved budget and credit counseling during the 180-day period preceding the filing of this petition. |
| ☐ Yes, and Exhibit C is attached and made a part of this petition.<br>☐ No | ☐ I/we request a waiver of the requirement to obtain budget and credit counseling prior to filing based on exigent circumstances. (Must attach certification describing.) |

### Information Regarding the Debtor (Check the Applicable Boxes)

**Venue** (Check any applicable box)

☐ Debtor has been domiciled or has had a residence, principal place of business, or principal assets in this District for 180 days immediately preceding the date of this petition or for a longer part of such 180 days than in any other District.

☐ There is a bankruptcy case concerning debtor's affiliate, general partner, or partnership pending in this District.

☐ Debtor is a debtor in a foreign proceeding and has its principal place of business or principal assets in the United States in this District, or has no principal place of business or assets in the United States but is a defendant in an action or proceeding [in a federal or state court] in this District, or the interests of the parties will be served in regard to the relief sought in this District.

### Statement by a Debtor Who Resides as a Tenant of Residential Property
*Check all applicable boxes.*

☐ Landlord has a judgment against the debtor for possession of debtor's residence. (If box checked, complete the following.)

_____
(Name of landlord that obtained judgment)

_____
(Address of landlord)

☐ Debtor claims that under applicable nonbankruptcy law, there are circumstances under which the debtor would be permitted to cure the entire monetary default that gave rise to the judgment for possession, after the judgment for possession was entered, and

☐ Debtor has included in this petition the deposit with the court of any rent that would become due during the 30-day period after the filing of the petition.

## DEBTOR'S VOLUNTARY BANKRUPTCY PETITION (OFFICIAL FORM 1)

| (Official Form 1) (10/05) | FORM B1, Page 3 |
|---|---|
| **Voluntary Petition** *(This page must be completed and filed in every case)* | Name of Debtor(s): |

### Signatures

| Signature(s) of Debtor(s) (Individual/Joint) | Signature of a Foreign Representative |
|---|---|
| I declare under penalty of perjury that the information provided in this petition is true and correct. [If petitioner is an individual whose debts are primarily consumer debts and has chosen to file under chapter 7] I am aware that I may proceed under chapter 7, 11, 12 or 13 of title 11, United States Code, understand the relief available under each such chapter, and choose to proceed under chapter 7. [If no attorney represents me and no bankruptcy petition preparer signs the petition] I have obtained and read the notice required by § 342(b) of the Bankruptcy Code.<br><br>I request relief in accordance with the chapter of title 11, United States Code, specified in this petition.<br><br>X_____<br>Signature of Debtor<br><br>X_____<br>Signature of Joint Debtor<br><br>_____<br>Telephone Number (If not represented by attorney)<br><br>_____<br>Date | I declare under penalty of perjury that the information provided in this petition is true and correct, that I am the foreign representative of a debtor in a foreign proceeding, and that I am authorized to file this petition.<br><br>(Check only one box.)<br><br>☐ I request relief in accordance with chapter 15 of title 11, United States Code. Certified copies of the documents required by § 1515 of title 11 are attached.<br><br>☐ Pursuant to § 1511 of title 11, United States Code, I request relief in accordance with the chapter of title 11 specified in this petition. A certified copy of the order granting recognition of the foreign main proceeding is attached.<br><br>X_____<br>(Signature of Foreign Representative)<br><br>_____<br>(Printed Name of Foreign Representative)<br><br>_____<br>Date |
| **Signature of Attorney**<br><br>X_____<br>Signature of Attorney for Debtor(s)<br><br>_____<br>Printed Name of Attorney for Debtor(s)<br><br>_____<br>Firm Name<br><br>_____<br>Address<br><br>_____<br>Telephone Number<br><br>_____<br>Date | **Signature of Non-Attorney Bankruptcy Petition Preparer**<br><br>I declare under penalty of perjury that: (1) I am a bankruptcy petition preparer as defined in 11 U.S.C. § 110; (2) I prepared this document for compensation and have provided the debtor with a copy of this document and the notices and information required under 11 U.S.C. §§ 110(b), 110(h), and 342(b); and, (3) if rules or guidelines have been promulgated pursuant to 11 U.S.C. § 110(h) setting a maximum fee for services chargeable by bankruptcy petition preparers, I have given the debtor notice of the maximum amount before preparing any document for filing for a debtor or accepting any fee from the debtor, as required in that section.Official Form 19B is attached.<br><br>_____<br>Printed Name and title, if any, of Bankruptcy Petition Preparer<br><br>_____<br>Social Security number (If the bankruptcy petition preparer is not an individual, state the Social Security number of the officer, principal, responsible person or partner of the bankruptcy petition preparer.)(Required by 11 U.S.C. § 110.) |
| **Signature of Debtor (Corporation/Partnership)**<br><br>I declare under penalty of perjury that the information provided in this petition is true and correct, and that I have been authorized to file this petition on behalf of the debtor.<br><br>The debtor requests relief in accordance with the chapter of title 11, United States Code, specified in this petition.<br><br>X_____<br>Signature of Authorized Individual<br><br>_____<br>Printed Name of Authorized Individual<br><br>_____<br>Title of Authorized Individual<br><br>_____<br>Date | Address<br><br>X_____<br><br>_____<br>Date<br><br>Signature of Bankruptcy Petition Preparer or officer, principal, responsible person,or partner whose social security number is provided above.<br><br>Names and Social Security numbers of all other individuals who prepared or assisted in preparing this document unless the bankruptcy petition preparer is not an individual:<br><br>If more than one person prepared this document, attach additional sheets conforming to the appropriate official form for each person.<br><br>*A bankruptcy petition preparer's failure to comply with the provisions of title 11 and the Federal Rules of Bankruptcy Procedure may result in fines or imprisonment or both 11 U.S.C. §110; 18 U.S.C. §156.* |

**Dealing with Debt**

# APPENDIX 15:
# CHAPTER 13 REPAYMENT PLAN

Name _____

Address _____

_____

Telephone _____ (FAX) _____

☐ Attorney for Debtor(s)    Attorney's
☐ Debtor(s) in Pro Se        State Bar I.D. No.
                             _____

### UNITED STATES BANKRUPTCY COURT
### CENTRAL DISTRICT OF CALIFORNIA

List all names including trade names used by Debtor(s) within last 6 years:

Chapter 13 Case No.:

### CHAPTER 13 PLAN

CREDITORS MEETING:
Date:
Time:
Place:
CONFIRMATION HEARING:
Date:
Time:
Place:

### NOTICE

This plan is proposed by the above debtor.* The debtor attests, under penalty of perjury, that the information stated in this plan is accurate. Creditors cannot vote on this plan. However, creditors may object to this plan being confirmed pursuant to 11 U.S.C. § 1324. Any objection must be in writing and must be filed with the court and served upon the debtor, debtor's attorney (if any), and the chapter 13 trustee not less than 8 days before the date set for the meeting of creditors. Unless an objection is filed and served, the court may confirm this chapter 13 plan. The plan, if confirmed, modifies the rights and duties of the debtor and creditors to the treatment provided in the plan as confirmed, with the following IMPORTANT EXCEPTIONS:

Holders of secured claims will be paid on their secured claims according to this plan unless the secured creditor files a proof of claim in a different amount than that provided in the plan. If a secured creditor files a proof of claim, that creditor will be paid according to that creditor's proof of claim, unless the court orders otherwise.

**HOLDERS OF ALL OTHER CLAIMS (INCLUDING PRIORITY CLAIMS, DEFICIENCY CLAIMS, ALL OTHER KINDS OF UNSECURED CLAIMS) MUST TIMELY FILE PROOFS OF CLAIM, OR THEY WILL NOT BE PAID ANY AMOUNT.** A debtor who confirms a chapter 13 plan may be eligible thereafter to receive a discharge of the debts to the extent specified in 11 U.S.C. § 1328.

*Any reference to the singular shall include the plural in the case of joint debtors.

This form is mandatory by Order of the United States Bankruptcy Court for the Central District of California.

Revised December 2003

F 3015-1.1

**Dealing with Debt**

# CHAPTER 13 REPAYMENT PLAN

Chapter 13 Plan (Rev. 12/03) - Page 2                                    2003 USBC, Central District of California

Case No.: _____

Debtor proposes the following chapter 13 plan and makes the following declarations:

I. **PROPERTIES AND FUTURE EARNINGS OR INCOME SUBJECT TO THE SUPERVISION AND CONTROL OF THE TRUSTEE:**

   Debtor submits the following to the supervision and control of the trustee:

   A. Payments by debtor of $_____ per month for _____ months. This monthly payment will begin within 30 days of the date the petition was filed.

   Debtor will pay _____% of the allowed claims of general unsecured creditors. If that percentage is less than 100%, the debtor will pay the plan payment stated in this plan for the full term of the plan.

   If the allowed general unsecured claims filed by creditors in this case total more than the amount stated in this plan, the debtor will: (1) obtain an order increasing the duration and/or amount of the monthly plan payment to provide for an amount sufficient to pay the above-stated percentage of the allowed claims filed by the unsecured creditors, or (2) obtain an order reducing the stated percentage. Failure to do one of the above may result in dismissal of the case.

   If the allowed general unsecured claims filed by creditors in this case total less than the amount stated in this plan, the above monthly plan payment may be sufficient to pay higher than the stated percent to general unsecured creditors. In this event, the debtor must still make the stated plan payment for the full plan term, and the trustee shall disburse said funds in payment of allowed unsecured claims up to payment of 100% thereof.

   B. Amounts necessary for the payment of postpetition claims allowed under 11 U.S.C. § 1305.

   C. Other property: _____
   *(specify property or indicate none)*

   Debtor will pay timely all post-confirmation tax liabilities directly to the appropriate taxing authorities.

II. **ORDER OF PAYMENTS; CLASSIFICATION AND TREATMENT OF CLAIMS:** Except as otherwise provided in the plan or by court order, the chapter 13 trustee shall disburse all available funds for the payment of claims as follows:

   1. **ORDER OF PAYMENTS:**

      1. The chapter 13 trustee's fee up to but not more than the amount accrued on actual payments made to date;

      2. Administrative expenses (including but not limited to attorney's fees) in an amount up to but not more than _____% of each plan payment until paid in full;

      3. Pro rata to all other classes up to the monthly amounts set forth in the plan, except that no payment shall be made on Class Five claims until all Class One claims have been paid in full.

---

This form is mandatory by Order of the United States Bankruptcy Court for the Central District of California.

Revised December 2003                                                         **F 3015-1.1**

Chapter 13 Plan (Rev. 12/03) - Page 3    2003 USBC, Central District of California

Case No.: _____

2. **CLASSIFICATION AND TREATMENT OF CLAIMS:**

   1. **CLASS ONE** - Allowed unsecured claims entitled to priority under 11 U.S.C. § 507. Debtor will pay Class One claims in full in deferred payments, provided a proof of claim has been filed, as follows:

      |   | AMOUNT OF PRIORITY CLAIM | MONTHLY PAYMENT | NUMBER OF PAYMENTS | TOTAL PAYMENT |
      |---|---|---|---|---|
      | a. Administrative Expenses | | | | |
      | (1) Trustee's Fee (estimated at 11% of plan payment amounts) | | | | |
      | (2) Attorney's Fees | $_____ | $_____ | #_____ | $_____ |
      | (3) Other | $_____ | $_____ | #_____ | $_____ |
      | b. Internal Revenue Service | $_____ | $_____ | #_____ | $_____ |
      | c. Franchise Tax Board | $_____ | $_____ | #_____ | $_____ |
      | d. Other _____ | $_____ | $_____ | #_____ | $_____ |
      | e. Other _____ | $_____ | $_____ | #_____ | $_____ |

   2. **CLASS TWO** - Claims secured solely by real property that is the debtor's PRINCIPAL RESIDENCE.

      a. Debtor will make all postpetition payments pursuant to the promissory note and deed of trust on the following claims on which the obligation matures **AFTER** the final payment is due under this plan:

         1. ☐ Directly to Trustee: _____
            *(name of creditor(s) here)*

         2. ☐ Directly to Creditor: _____
            *(name of creditor(s) here)*

      b. Debtor will make all postpetition payments pursuant to the promissory note and deed of trust on the following claims on which the obligation matures **BEFORE** the final payment is due under this plan: _____
         _____ *(name of creditor(s) here).*

      c. Debtor will cure all prepetition arrearages through the plan payment as set forth below:

      | Name of Creditor and Last Four Digits of Loan Number | AMOUNT OF ARREARAGES | INTEREST RATE | MONTHLY PAYMENT | NUMBER OF MONTHS | TOTAL PAYMENT |
      |---|---|---|---|---|---|
      | Name _____ Loan No. _____ Cure of default | $_____ | _____% | $_____ | #_____ | $_____ |
      | Name _____ Loan No. _____ Cure of default | $_____ | _____% | $_____ | #_____ | $_____ |
      | Name _____ Loan No. _____ Cure of default | $_____ | _____% | $_____ | #_____ | $_____ |
      | Name _____ Loan No. _____ Cure of default | $_____ | _____% | $_____ | #_____ | $_____ |

This form is mandatory by Order of the United States Bankruptcy Court for the Central District of California.

Revised December 2003                              F 3015-1.1

# CHAPTER 13 REPAYMENT PLAN

Chapter 13 Plan (Rev. 12/03) - Page 4            2003 USBC, Central District of California

Case No.: _____

d. Pursuant to Sections 1322(c)(2) and 1325(a)(5), Debtor will pay the following claim(s) on which the obligation matures **BEFORE** the final payment is due under this plan as follows:

| NAME OF CREDITOR | AMOUNT | INTEREST RATE | MONTHLY PAYMENT | NUMBER OF MONTHS | TOTAL PAYMENT |
|---|---|---|---|---|---|
| _____ | $_____ | ____% | $_____ | #_____ | $_____ |
| _____ | $_____ | ____% | $_____ | #_____ | $_____ |
| _____ | $_____ | ____% | $_____ | #_____ | $_____ |

Each creditor will retain its lien until its secured claim is paid in full or it is otherwise satisfied by surrender, agreement, or order of the court.

3. **CLASS THREE** - Secured claims on real or personal property which are paid in full during the term of the plan, including but not limited to a claim which is not secured solely by a security interest in the debtor's principal residence. Class Three claims will be paid in monthly payments as set forth below. Debtor is the owner of the property serving as collateral, is aware of its condition and, where the secured claim is less than the amount of the debt, believes its value is as set forth below under the heading "Amount of Secured Claim." The value as of the effective date of the plan of the series of payments to be distributed under the plan on account of each secured claim provided for by the plan is equal to the allowed amount of such claim. Any unsecured amount resulting from a deficiency in the value of the collateral is included in Class Five, or if appropriate, in Class One.

| Name of Creditor and Last Four Digits of Loan Number | TOTAL AMOUNT OF CLAIM | AMOUNT OF SECURED CLAIM | INTEREST RATE ON SECURED CLAIM | AMOUNT OF UNSECURED CLAIM | MONTHLY PAYMENT | TOTAL NUMBER OF PAYMENTS | TOTAL PAYMENT |
|---|---|---|---|---|---|---|---|
| Name _____ Loan No. _____ | $_____ | $_____ | ____% | $_____ | $_____ | #_____ | $_____ |
| Name _____ Loan No. _____ | $_____ | $_____ | ____% | $_____ | $_____ | #_____ | $_____ |
| Name _____ Loan No. _____ | $_____ | $_____ | ____% | $_____ | $_____ | #_____ | $_____ |
| Name _____ Loan No. _____ | $_____ | $_____ | ____% | $_____ | $_____ | #_____ | $_____ |
| Name _____ Loan No. _____ | $_____ | $_____ | ____% | $_____ | $_____ | #_____ | $_____ |

Each creditor will retain its lien until (1) if oversecured, its secured claim is paid in full, or (2) if undersecured, its secured claim is paid in full and the debtor receives a discharge under chapter 13.

---

This form is mandatory by Order of the United States Bankruptcy Court for the Central District of California.

*Revised December 2003*        **F 3015-1.1**

Chapter 13 Plan (Rev. 12/03) - Page 5                              2003 USBC, Central District of California

Case No.: _____

4. **CLASS FOUR** - Claims secured by real or personal property other than the debtor's principal residence for which arrearages are paid as part of the plan payment and for which the ongoing obligation will be paid according to the terms of the agreement to the party stated below. The value as of the effective date of the plan of the series of payments to be distributed under the plan on account of each secured claim provided for by the plan is equal to the allowed amount of such claim. Defaults will be cured using the interest rate set forth below. (If more than two creditors, attach separate exhibits.)

| Name of Creditor and Last Four Digits of Loan Number | AMOUNT OF ARREARAGES | INTEREST RATE ON ARREARAGES | MONTHLY PAYMENT | NUMBER OF MONTHS | TOTAL PAYMENT |
|---|---|---|---|---|---|

Name _____

Loan No. _____
1) Cure of default        $_____    _____%    $_____    #_____    $_____
2) Regular monthly payment                            $_____    #_____    $_____

☐ To the trustee as part of the plan payment during the life of the plan and thereafter directly to the creditor.

☐ Directly to the creditor

Name _____

Loan No. _____
1) Cure of default        $_____    _____%    $_____    #_____    $_____
2) Regular monthly payment                            $_____    #_____    $_____

☐ To the trustee as part of the plan payment during the life of the plan and thereafter directly to the creditor.

☐ Directly to the creditor

Each creditor will retain its lien until (1) if oversecured, its secured claim is paid in full, or (2) if undersecured, its secured claim is paid in full and the debtor receives a discharge under chapter 13.

5. **CLASS FIVE** - Non-priority Unsecured Claims. Debtor estimates that non-priority general unsecured claims total the sum of $_____. Class Five claims will be paid as follows, subject to the terms of IA herein:

(Check one box only.)

☐ Class Five claims (including allowed unsecured amounts from Class Three) are of one class and will be paid pro rata at ____% of such claims. Unless the plan provides for payment of 100% to unsecured creditors, the debtor will pay all disposable income to the trustee for at least 36 months and will submit statements of income to the trustee on a semi-annual/annual basis. The amount of income shall be reviewed by the trustee who may petition the court to increase the monthly payments for cause.

OR

---

This form is mandatory by Order of the United States Bankruptcy Court for the Central District of California.

Revised December 2003                                                                   **F 3015-1.1**

**Dealing with Debt**                                                                        133

# CHAPTER 13 REPAYMENT PLAN

Chapter 13 Plan (Rev. 12/03) - Page 6  2003 USBC, Central District of California

Case No.: _____

☐ Class Five claims will be divided into subclasses as shown on the attached Exhibit ____ and paid pro rata in each subclass as indicated therein. The Plan provides the same treatment for each claim within each subclass of Class Five. The claims of each subclass are substantially similar and the division into subclasses does not discriminate unfairly.

6. **CLASS SIX** - Postpetition claims under 11 U.S.C. § 1305. Postpetition claims allowed under 11 U.S.C. § 1305 will be paid in full in equal monthly installments commencing no later than 30 days after entry of an order allowing such claims and concluding on the date of the last payment under the plan, provided sufficient funds are available under the plan or amended plan.

III. **COMPARISON WITH CHAPTER 7** - The value as of the effective date of the plan of property to be distributed under the plan on account of each allowed claim is not less than the amount that would be paid on such claim if the estate of the debtor were liquidated under chapter 7 of the Bankruptcy Code on such date. The percentage distribution to general unsecured creditors in chapter 7 would be (estimate) _____ %.

IV. **PLAN ANALYSIS** - TOTAL PAYMENT PROVIDED FOR UNDER THE PLAN

```
CLASS ONE
    Unpaid attorney's fee  . . . . . . . . . . . . . . . . . . . . . . . . . . . . . . . . . . . . . . . .  $_____
    Internal Revenue Service  . . . . . . . . . . . . . . . . . . . . . . . . . . . . . . . . . . . .  $_____
    Franchise Tax Board  . . . . . . . . . . . . . . . . . . . . . . . . . . . . . . . . . . . . . . . .  $_____
    Other  . . . . . . . . . . . . . . . . . . . . . . . . . . . . . . . . . . . . . . . . . . . . . . . . . . . . . .  $_____
    Other  . . . . . . . . . . . . . . . . . . . . . . . . . . . . . . . . . . . . . . . . . . . . . . . . . . . . . .  $_____
CLASS TWO  . . . . . . . . . . . . . . . . . . . . . . . . . . . . . . . . . . . . . . . . . . . . . . . . . .  $_____
CLASS THREE  . . . . . . . . . . . . . . . . . . . . . . . . . . . . . . . . . . . . . . . . . . . . . . . .  $_____
CLASS FOUR  . . . . . . . . . . . . . . . . . . . . . . . . . . . . . . . . . . . . . . . . . . . . . . . . .  $_____
CLASS FIVE  . . . . . . . . . . . . . . . . . . . . . . . . . . . . . . . . . . . . . . . . . . . . . . . . . .  $_____
    SUB-TOTAL  . . . . . . . . . . . . . . . . . . . . . . . . . . . . . . . . . . . . . . . . . . . . . . . .  $_____
    TRUSTEE'S FEES (Estimate 11% unless advised otherwise.)  . . . . . . . . . . . . . . . . . . $_____
    TOTAL PAYMENTS  . . . . . . . . . . . . . . . . . . . . . . . . . . . . . . . . . . . . . . . . . . .  $_____
```

V. **ENLARGEMENT OF TIME FOR PAYMENTS**

If the plan provides for payments over a period of more than 36 months, cause exists as follows:

_____  The plan proposes to pay at least 70% of unsecured claims.

_____  Other: _____

VI. **DEBTOR'S ABILITY TO MAKE PAYMENTS AND COMPLY WITH BANKRUPTCY CODE**

Debtor will be able to make all payments and comply with all provisions of the plan, based upon the availability to the debtor of the income and property the debtor proposes to use to complete the plan.

This plan complies with the provisions of chapter 13 and all other applicable provisions of the Bankruptcy Code. Any fee, charge, or amount required to be paid under the United States Code or required by the plan to be paid before confirmation has been paid or will be paid prior to confirmation. The plan has been proposed in good faith and not by any means forbidden by law.

---

This form is mandatory by Order of the United States Bankruptcy Court for the Central District of California.

Revised December 2003

F 3015-1.1

Chapter 13 Plan (Rev. 12/03) - Page 7  2003 USBC, Central District of California

Case No.: _____

## VII. OTHER PROVISIONS

A. Debtor rejects the following executory contracts and unexpired leases: _____

_____
_____

B. Debtor assumes the executory contracts or unexpired leases set forth in this section. As to each contract or lease assumed, any defaults therein and debtor's proposal for cure of said default(s) is described. Evidence satisfying all requirements for assumption is provided in a separately filed pleading.

_____
_____
_____
_____

C. In addition to the payments specified in Section II herein, the debtor will make regular payments directly to the following:

_____
_____
_____

D. Debtor hereby surrenders the following personal or real property: _____

_____
_____

E. Miscellaneous provisions *(specify)*: _____

_____
_____

F. The trustee is authorized to disburse funds after the date of confirmation in open court.

---

This form is mandatory by Order of the United States Bankruptcy Court for the Central District of California.

Revised December 2003

**F 3015-1.1**

**Dealing with Debt** 135

CHAPTER 13 REPAYMENT PLAN

Chapter 13 Plan (Rev. 12/03) - Page 8     2003 USBC, Central District of California

Case No.: _____

VIII.   **REVESTMENT OF PROPERTY**

Property of the estate shall not revest in the debtor until such time as a discharge is granted or the case is dismissed. Revestment shall be subject to all liens and encumbrances in existence when the case was filed, except those liens avoided by court order or extinguished by operation of law. In the event the case is converted to a case under chapter 7, 11, or 12 of the Bankruptcy Code, the property of the estate shall vest in accordance with applicable law. After confirmation of the plan, the chapter 13 trustee shall have no further authority or fiduciary duty regarding use, sale, or refinance of property of the estate, except to respond to any motion for proposed use, sale, or refinance as required by the Chapter 13 General Order of this court. Prior to any discharge or dismissal, the debtor must seek approval of the court to purchase, sell, or refinance real property.

Dated: _____     _____
                                            *Attorney for Debtor(s)*

I declare under penalty of perjury that the foregoing is true and correct.

Executed at _____, California     _____
                                                    *Debtor*

Executed on: _____         _____
                                              *Joint Debtor*

---

This form is mandatory by Order of the United States Bankruptcy Court for the Central District of California.

*Revised December 2003*                                        **F 3015-1.1**

# APPENDIX 16:
# FEDERAL EXEMPTIONS UNDER §522(D) OF THE BANKRUPTCY CODE

1. Debtor's aggregate interest, not to exceed $18,450 in value, in real property or personal property that the debtor, or a dependent of the debtor, uses as a residence, in a cooperative that owns property that the debtor or a dependent of the debtor uses as a residence, or in a burial plot for the debtor or a dependent of the debtor.

2. The debtor's interest, not to exceed $2,950 in value, in one motor vehicle.

3. The debtor's interest, not to exceed $425 in value in any particular item or $9,850 in aggregate value, in household furnishings, household goods, wearing apparel, appliances, books, animals, crops, or musical instruments, that are held primarily for the personal, family, or household use of the debtor or a dependent of the debtor.

4. The debtor's aggregate interest, not to exceed $1,225 in value, in jewelry held primarily for the personal, family, or household use of the debtor or a dependent of the debtor.

5. The debtor's aggregate interest in any property, not to exceed in value $975 plus up to $9,250 of any unused amount of the exemption provided under paragraph (1) of this subsection.

6. The debtor's aggregate interest, not to exceed $1,850 in value, in any implements, professional books, or tools, of the trade of the debtor or the trade of a dependent of the debtor.

7. Any unmatured life insurance contract owned by the debtor, other than a credit life insurance contract.

8. The debtor's aggregate interest, not to exceed in value $9,850 less any amount of property of the estate transferred in the manner specified in section 542(d) of this title, in any accrued dividend or interest

under, or loan value of, any un-matured life insurance contract owned by the debtor under which the insured is the debtor or an individual of whom the debtor is a dependent.

9. Professionally prescribed health aids for the debtor or a dependent of the debtor.

10. The debtor's right to receive:

>(a) A social security benefit, unemployment compensation, or a local public assistance benefit;

>(b) A veterans' benefit;

>(c) A disability, illness, or unemployment benefit;

>(d) Alimony, support, or separate maintenance, to the extent reasonably necessary for the support of the debtor and any dependent of the debtor;

>(e) A payment under a stock bonus, pension, profit-sharing, annuity, or similar plan or contract on account of illness, disability, death, age, or length of service, to the extent reasonably necessary for the support of the debtor and any dependent of the debtor, unless: (i) such plan or contract was established by or under the auspices of an insider that employed the debtor at the time the debtor's rights under such plan or contract arose; (ii) such payment is on account of age or length of service; and (iii) such plan or contract does not qualify under section 401(a), 403(a), 403(b), 408, or 409 of the Internal Revenue Code of 1986 (26 U.S.C. 401(a), 403(a), 403(b), 408, or 409).

11. The debtor's right to receive, or property that is traceable to:

>(a) An award under a crime victim's reparation law;

>(b) A payment on account of the wrongful death of an individual of whom the debtor was a dependent, to the extent reasonably necessary for the support of the debtor and any dependent of the debtor;

>(c) A payment under a life insurance contract that insured the life of an individual of whom the debtor was a dependent on the date of such individual's death, to the extent reasonably necessary for the support of the debtor and any dependent of the debtor;

>(d) A payment, not to exceed $18,450, on account of personal bodily injury, not including pain and suffering or compensation for actual pecuniary loss, of the debtor or an individual of whom the debtor is a dependent; or

>(e) A payment in compensation of loss of future earnings of the debtor or an individual of whom the debtor is or was a dependent, to the extent reasonably necessary for the support of the debtor and any dependent of the debtor.

# APPENDIX 17:
# TABLE OF STATE STATUTES GOVERNING BANKRUPTCY EXEMPTIONS

| STATE | STATUTE |
|---|---|
| Alabama | Alabama Code §6-10-2 (homestead); §6-10-5 (burial place); §6-10-6 (personal property) |
| Alaska | Alaska Statutes §09.38.010 (homestead); §09.38.017 (retirement benefits); §§09.38.015 et. seq. (personal property) |
| Arizona | Arizona Revised Statutes Annotated §33-101 (homestead); §§33-1121 et. seq. (personal property) |
| Arkansas | Arkansas Statutes Annotated §§16-66-210 and 16-66-218b (homestead); §16-22-218a (property); §16-66-218b (personal property) |
| California | California Civil Code §704.730 (homestead); §§704.010 et. seq. (personal property) |
| Colorado | Colorado Revised Statutes §§38-41-201 et. seq. (homestead); §13-54-102 (personal property) |
| Connecticut | Connecticut General Statutes Annotated §52-352b (personal property) |
| Delaware | Delaware Code Annotated Title 10 §§4902 et. seq. (personal property) |
| District of Columbia | D.C.Code Annotated §15-501 (personal property) |
| Florida | Florida Const. Art. X§4 (homestead/personal property); Florida Statutes §§222.11 et. seq. (miscellaneous) |

**Dealing with Debt**

TABLE OF STATE STATUTES GOVERNING BANKRUPTCY EXEMPTIONS

| | |
|---|---|
| Georgia | Georgia Code Annotated §§44-13-1 et. seq. (real/personal property); §44-13-100 (another option) |
| Hawaii | Hawaii Revised Statutes §651-92 (homestead); §651-121 (personal property) |
| Idaho | Idaho Code §§55-1001 et. seq. (homestead); §§11-603 et. seq. (personal property) |
| Illinois | Illinois Annotated Statutes Chapter 110 §§12-901 et. seq. (homestead); §§12-1001 et. seq. (personal property) |
| Indiana | Indiana Code Annotated §34-2-28-1 (real/personal property) |
| Iowa | Iowa Code Annotated §§561.1 et. seq. (homestead); §§627.1 et. seq. (personal property) |
| Kansas | Kansas Constitution Art. 15§9 and Kansas Statutes Annotated §§60-2301 et. seq. (homestead); §60-2304 (personal property) |
| Kentucky | Kentucky Revised Statutes Annotated §§427.060 et. seq. (homestead); §§4287.010 et. seq. (personal property) |
| Louisiana | Louisiana Revised Statutes Annotated §20:1 (homestead); §13:3881 (personal property) |
| Maine | Maine Revised Statutes Annotated Title 14 §4422 (homestead/personal property) |
| Maryland | Annotated Code of Maryland §11-504 (personal property) |
| Massachusetts | Massachusetts General Laws Annotated, Chapter 188 §§1 et. seq. (homestead); Chapter 235 §34 (personal property) |
| Michigan | Michigan Constitution Article X §3 and Michigan Compiled Laws Annotated §27A.6023(h) (homestead); §600.6023 (personal property) |
| Minnesota | Minnesota Statutes Annotated §§510.01 et. seq. (homestead); §550.37 (personal property) |
| Mississippi | Mississippi Code Annotated §§85-3-21 et. seq. (homestead); §85-3-1 (other property) |

## TABLE OF STATE STATUTES GOVERNING BANKRUPTCY EXEMPTIONS

| | |
|---|---|
| Missouri | Missouri Annotated Statutes §§513.475 et seq. (homestead); §§513.430 et. seq. (personal property) |
| Montana | Montana Code Annotated §§70-32-101 et. seq. (homestead); §§25-13-608 et. seq. (personal property) |
| Nebraska | Nebraska Revised Statutes §§40-101 et. seq. (homestead); §§25-1552 et. seq. (personal property) |
| Nevada | Nevada Constitution Art. 4 §30 and Nevada Revised Statutes Annotated §§115.005 et. seq. (homestead); Nevada Constitution Art. 1 §14 and Nevada Revised Statutes Annotated §§21.090 et. seq. (personal property) |
| New Hampshire | New Hampshire Revised Statutes Annotated §480:1 (homestead); §511:2 (personal property) |
| New Jersey | New Jersey Statutes Annotated §2A:17-19 (personal property) |
| New Mexico | New Mexico Statutes Annotated §42-10-9 (homestead); §§42-10-1 et. seq. (personal property) |
| New York | New York Civil Practice Law and Rules §5206 (homestead); §5205 (personal property); Debtor and Creditor Law §282 et. seq. (bankruptcy exemptions) |
| North Carolina | North Carolina Constitution Art. X §2 and North Carolina General Statutes §§1C-1601 et. seq. (homestead); North Carolina Constitution Art. X §1 and North Carolina General Statutes §1C-1601 (personal property) |
| North Dakota | North Dakota Cent. Code §§47-18-01 et. seq. (homestead); §§28-22-02 et. seq. (personal property) |
| Ohio | Ohio Revised Code Annotated §2329.66 (homestead/personal property) |
| Oklahoma | Oklahoma Statutes Annotated Title 31 §2 (homestead); Title 31 §1 (other property) |
| Oregon | Oregon Revised Statutes §§23.240 et. seq. (homestead); §23.160 (personal property) |
| Pennsylvania | 23 Pennsylvania Cons. Statutes Annotated 42 §8124 (personal property); 42 §8123 (general monetary) |

**Dealing with Debt**

# TABLE OF STATE STATUTES GOVERNING BANKRUPTCY EXEMPTIONS

| | |
|---|---|
| Rhode Island | Rhode Island General Laws §9-26-4 (personal property) |
| South Carolina | South Carolina Code Annotated §15-41-30(1) (homestead); §15-42-30 (personal property) |
| South Dakota | South Dakota Codified Laws Annotated §43-45-3 and §§43-31-1 et. seq. (homestead); §§43-45-1 et. seq. (personal property) |
| Tennessee | Tennessee State Constitution Art. XI §11 and Tennessee Code Annotated §§26-2-301 et. seq. (homestead); §§26-2-102 et. seq. (personal property) |
| Texas | Texas Codes Annotated §§41.001 et. seq. (homestead); §§42.001 et. seq. (personal property) |
| Utah | Utah Constitution Art. XXII §1 and Utah Code Annotated §§78-23-3 et. seq. (homestead); §§78-23-5 et. seq. (personal property) |
| Vermont | Vermont Statutes Annotated Title 27 §§101 et. seq. (homestead); Title 27 §2740 (personal property) |
| Virginia | Virginia Code Annotated §§34-4 et. seq. (homestead); §34-26 (personal property) |
| Washington | Washington Revised Code Annotated §§6.13.010 et. seq. (homestead); §6.15.010 (personal property) |
| West Virginia | West Virginia Code §§38-9-1 et. seq. (homestead); §§38-8-1 et. seq. (personal property); 38-10-4 (bankruptcy exemptions) |
| Wisconsin | Wisconsin Statutes Annotated §815.20 and §990.01(14) (homestead); §815.18 (personal property) |
| Wyoming | Wyoming Constitution Art. 19 §9 and Wyoming Statutes Annotated §§1-20-101 et. seq. (homestead); §§1-20-105 et. seq. (personal property) |

# APPENDIX 18:
# PROOF OF CLAIM

Form B10 (Official Form 10) (10/05)

| United States Bankruptcy Court    Central District of California | **PROOF OF CLAIM** |
|---|---|
| Name of Debtor | Case Number |

**NOTE:** This form should not be used to make a claim for an administrative expense arising after the commencement of the case. A "request" for payment of an administrative expense may be filed pursuant to 11 U.S.C. § 503.

| Name of Creditor (The person or other entity to whom the debtor owes money or property): | ❑ Check box if you are aware that anyone else has filed a proof of claim relating to your claim. Attach copy of statement giving particulars. | |
|---|---|---|
| Name and address where notices should be sent: <br><br> Telephone number: | ❑ Check box if you have never received any notices from the bankruptcy court in this case. <br><br> ❑ Check box if the address differs from the address on the envelope sent to you by the court. | This space is for Court use only. |
| Last four digits of account or other number by which creditor identifies debtor: | Check here   ❑ replaces <br> if this claim   ❑ amends   a previously filed claim, dated: _____ | |

**1. Basis for Claim**
- ❑ Goods sold
- ❑ Services performed
- ❑ Money loaned
- ❑ Personal injury/wrongful death
- ❑ Taxes
- ❑ Other _____

- ❑ Retiree benefits as defined in 11 U.S.C. § 1114(a)
- ❑ Wages, salaries, and compensation (Fill out below)
  Last four digits of your Social Security number: _____
  Unpaid compensation for services performed
  from _____ to _____
       (date)      (date)

**2. Date debt was incurred:**      **3. If court judgment, date obtained:**

**4. Total Amount of Claim at Time Case Filed:**   $_____   $_____   $_____   $_____
                                     (unsecured)    (secured)    (priority)    (Total)

If all or part of your claim is secured or entitled to priority, also complete Item 5 or 7 below.
❑ Check this box if claim includes interest or other charges in addition to the principal amount of the claim. Attach itemized statement of all interest or additional charges.

**5. Secured Claim.**
❑ Check this box if your claim is secured by collateral (including a right of setoff).

Brief Description of Collateral:
❑ Real Estate    ❑ Motor Vehicle
❑ Other _____

Value of Collateral: $_____

Amount of arrearage and other charges *at time case filed* included in secured claim, if any $_____

**6. Unsecured Nonpriority Claim.** $_____
❑ Check this box if (a) there is no collateral or lien securing your claim, or (b) your claim exceeds the value of the property securing it or (c) none or only part of your claim is entitled to priority.

**7. Unsecured Priority Claim.**
❑ Check this box if you have an unsecured priority claim, all or part of which is entitled to priority.
Amount entitled to priority $_____
Specify the priority of the claim:
❑ Wages, salaries or commissions (up to $10,000),* earned within 180 days before filing of the bankruptcy petition or cessation of the debtor's business, whichever is earlier - 11 U.S.C. § 507(a)(4).
❑ Contributions to an employee benefit plan - 11 U.S.C. § 507(a)(5).
❑ Up to $2,225* of deposits toward purchase, lease or rental of property or services for personal, family, or household use - 11 U.S.C. § 507(a)(7).
❑ Domestic support obligations under - 11 U.S.C. § 507(a)(1)(A) or (a)(1)(B).
❑ Taxes or penalties owed to governmental units - 11 U.S.C. § 507(a)(8).
❑ Other - Specify applicable paragraph of 11 U.S.C. § 507(a)(____).
*Amounts are subject to adjustment on 4/1/07 and every 3 years thereafter with respect to cases commenced on or after the date of adjustment. $10,000 and 180-day limits apply to cases filed on or after 4/20/05. Pub. L. 109-8*

| 8. | **Credits:** The amount of all payments on this claim has been credited and deducted for the purpose of making this proof of claim. | This space is for Court use only. |
|---|---|---|
| 9. | **Supporting Documents:** *Attach copies of supporting documents,* such as promissory notes, purchase orders, invoices, itemized statements of running accounts, contracts, court judgments, mortgages, security agreements, and evidence of perfection of lien. DO NOT SEND ORIGINAL DOCUMENTS. If the documents are not available, explain. If the documents are voluminous, attach a summary. | |
| 10. | **Date-Stamped Copy:** To receive an acknowledgment of the filing of your claim, enclose a stamped, self-addressed envelope and copy of this proof of claim. | |
| Date | Sign and print the name and title, if any, of the creditor or other person authorized to file this claim (attach copy of power of attorney, if any): | |

*Penalty for presenting fraudulent claim: Fine of up to $500,000 or imprisonment for up to 5 years, or both. 18 U.S.C. §§ 152 and 3571.*

**Dealing with Debt**

# PROOF OF CLAIM

Form B10 (Official Form 10) (10/05)

## INSTRUCTIONS FOR PROOF OF CLAIM FORM

The instructions and definitions below are general explanations of the law. In particular types of cases or circumstances, such as bankruptcy cases that are not filed voluntarily by a debtor, there may be exceptions to these general rules.

------ DEFINITIONS ------

**Debtor**
The person, corporation, or other entity that has filed a bankruptcy case is called the debtor.

**Creditor**
A creditor is any person, corporation, or other entity to whom the debtor owed a debt on the date that the bankruptcy case was filed.

**Proof of Claim**
A form telling the bankruptcy court how much the debtor owed a creditor at the time the bankruptcy case was filed (the amount of the creditor's claim). This form must be filed with the clerk of the bankruptcy court where the bankruptcy case was filed.

**Secured Claim**
A claim is a secured claim to the extent that the creditor has a lien on property of the debtor (collateral) that gives the creditor the right to be paid from that property before creditors who do not have liens on the property.

Examples of liens are a mortgage on real estate and a security interest in a car, truck, boat, television set, or other item of property. A lien may have been obtained through a court proceeding before the bankruptcy case began; in some states a court judgment is a lien. In addition, to the extent a creditor also owes money to the debtor (has a right of setoff), the creditor's claim may be a secured claim. (See also Unsecured Claim.)

**Unsecured Claim**
If a claim is not a secured claim it is an unsecured claim. A claim may be partly secured and partly unsecured if the property on which a creditor has a lien is not worth enough to pay the creditor in full.

**Unsecured Priority Claim**
Certain types of unsecured claims are given priority, so they are to be paid in bankruptcy cases before most other unsecured claims (if there is sufficient money or property available to pay these claims). The most common types of priority claims are listed on the proof of claim form. Unsecured claims that are not specifically given priority status by the bankruptcy laws are classified as Unsecured Nonpriority claims.

### Items to be completed in Proof of Claim form (if not already filled in)

**Court, Name of Debtor, and Case Number:**
Fill in the name of the federal judicial district where the bankruptcy case was filed (for example: Central District of California), the name of the debtor in the bankruptcy case, and the bankruptcy case number. If you received a notice of the case from the court, all of this information is near the top of the notice.

**Information about Creditor:**
Complete the section giving the name, address, and telephone number of the creditor to whom the debtor owes money or property, and the debtor's account number, if any. If anyone else has already filed a proof of claim relating to this debt, if you never received notices from the bankruptcy court about this case, if your address differs from that to which the court sent notice, or if this proof of claim replaces or changes a proof of claim that was already filed, check the appropriate box on the form.

1. **Basis for Claim:**
   Check the type of debt for which the proof of claim is being filed. If the type of debt is not listed, check "Other" and briefly describe the type of debt. If you were an employee of the debtor, fill in the last four digits of your Social Security number and the dates of work for which you were not paid.

2. **Date Debt Incurred:**
   Fill in the date when the debt first was owed by the debtor.

3. **Court Judgments:**
   If you have a court judgment for this debt, state the date the court entered the judgment.

4. **Total Amount of Claim at Time Case Filed:**
   Fill in the total amount of the entire claim. If interest or other charges in addition to the principal amount of the claim are included, check the appropriate place on the form and attach an itemization of the interest and charges.

5. **Secured Claim:**
   Check the appropriate place if the claim is a secured claim. You must state the type and value of property that is collateral for the claim, attach copies of the documentation of your lien, and state the amount past due on the claim as of the date the bankruptcy case was filed. A claim may be partly secured and partly unsecured. (See DEFINITIONS, above.)

6. **Unsecured Nonpriority Claim:**
   Check the appropriate place if you have an unsecured nonpriority claim, sometimes referred to as a "general unsecured claim." (See DEFINITIONS, above.) If your claim is partly secured and partly unsecured, state here the amount that is unsecured. If part of your claim is entitled to priority, state here the amount **not** entitled to priority.

7. **Unsecured Priority Claim:**
   Check the appropriate place if you have an unsecured priority claim, and state the amount entitled to priority. (See DEFINITIONS, above.) A claim may be partly priority and partly nonpriority if, for example, the claim is for more than the amount given priority by the law. Check the appropriate place to specify the type of priority claim.

8. **Credits:**
   By signing this proof of claim, you are stating under oath that in calculating the amount of your claim you have given the debtor credit for all payments received from the debtor.

9. **Supporting Documents:**
   You must attach to this proof of claim form copies of documents that show the debtor owes the debt claimed or, if the documents are too lengthy, a summary of those documents. If documents are not available, you must attach an explanation of why they are not available.

# APPENDIX 19:
# REAFFIRMATION AGREEMENT

B 240 - Reaffirmation Agreement
(10/05))

United States Bankruptcy Court<br>_____District of _____

In re _____,     Case No._____
               Debtor     Chapter _____

### REAFFIRMATION AGREEMENT

*[Indicate all documents included in this filing by checking each applicable box.]*

☐ Part A: Disclosures, Instructions, and Notice to Debtor (Pages 1 - 5)
☐ Part B: Reaffirmation Agreement
☐ Part C: Certification by Debtor's Attorney
☐ Part D: Debtor's Statement in Support of Reaffirmation Agreement
☐ Part E: Motion for Court Approval
☐ Proposed Order Approving Reaffirmation Agreement

☐ *[Check this box if]* Creditor is a Credit Union as defined in §19(b)(1)(a)(iv) of the Federal Reserve Act

**PART A: DISCLOSURE STATEMENT, INSTRUCTIONS AND NOTICE TO DEBTOR**

    **1. DISCLOSURE STATEMENT**

*Before Agreeing to Reaffirm a Debt, Review These Important Disclosures*:

### SUMMARY OF REAFFIRMATION AGREEMENT

This Summary is made pursuant to the requirements of the Bankruptcy Code.

### AMOUNT REAFFIRMED

| | | |
|---|---|---|
| a. | The amount of debt you have agreed to reaffirm: | $_____ |
| b. | All fees and costs accrued as of the date of this disclosure statement, related to the amount of debt shown in a., above: | $_____ |
| c. | The total amount you have agreed to reaffirm (Debt and fees and costs) (Add lines a. and b.): | $_____ |

*Your credit agreement may obligate you to pay additional amounts which may come due after the date of this disclosure. Consult your credit agreement.*

P. 2

**REAFFIRMATION AGREEMENT**

### ANNUAL PERCENTAGE RATE

*[The annual percentage rate can be disclosed in different ways, depending on the type of debt.]*

    a. If the debt is an extension of "credit" under an "open end credit plan," as those terms are defined in § 103 of the Truth in Lending Act, such as a credit card, the creditor may disclose the annual percentage rate shown in (I) below or, to the extent this rate is not readily available or not applicable, the simple interest rate shown in (ii) below, or both.

    (I) The Annual Percentage Rate disclosed, or that would have been disclosed, to the debtor in the most recent periodic statement prior to entering into the reaffirmation agreement described in Part B below or, if no such periodic statement was given to the debtor during the prior six months, the annual percentage rate as it would have been so disclosed at the time of the disclosure statement: _____%.

— And/Or ---

    (ii) The simple interest rate applicable to the amount reaffirmed as of the date this disclosure statement is given to the debtor: _____%. If different simple interest rates apply to different balances included in the amount reaffirmed, the amount of each balance and the rate applicable to it are:

    $_____ @ _____%;
    $_____ @ _____%;
    $_____ @ _____%.

    b. If the debt is an extension of credit other than under than an open end credit plan, the creditor may disclose the annual percentage rate shown in (I) below, or, to the extent this rate is not readily available or not applicable, the simple interest rate shown in (ii) below, or both.

    (I) The Annual Percentage Rate under §128(a)(4) of the Truth in Lending Act, as disclosed to the debtor in the most recent disclosure statement given to the debtor prior to entering into the reaffirmation agreement with respect to the debt or, if no such disclosure statement was given to the debtor, the annual percentage rate as it would have been so disclosed: _____%.

— And/Or ---

    (ii) The simple interest rate applicable to the amount reaffirmed as of the date this disclosure statement is given to the debtor: _____%. If different simple interest rates apply to different balances included in the amount reaffirmed,

P. 3

the amount of each balance and the rate applicable to it are:
$ _____ @ _____%;
$ _____ @ _____%;
$ _____ @ _____%.

c. If the underlying debt transaction was disclosed as a variable rate transaction on the most recent disclosure given under the Truth in Lending Act:

The interest rate on your loan may be a variable interest rate which changes from time to time, so that the annual percentage rate disclosed here may be higher or lower.

d. If the reaffirmed debt is secured by a security interest or lien, which has not been waived or determined to be void by a final order of the court, the following items or types of items of the debtor's goods or property remain subject to such security interest or lien in connection with the debt or debts being reaffirmed in the reaffirmation agreement described in Part B.

Item or Type of Item                Original Purchase Price or Original Amount of Loan

*Optional*---At the election of the creditor, a repayment schedule using one or a combination of the following may be provided:

**Repayment Schedule:**

Your first payment in the amount of $_____ is due on _____(date), but the future payment amount may be different. Consult your reaffirmation agreement or credit agreement, as applicable.

---*Or*---

Your payment schedule will be: _____(number) payments in the amount of $_____ each, payable (monthly, annually, weekly, etc.) on the _____ (day) of each _____ ( week, month, etc.), unless altered later by mutual agreement in writing.

---*Or*---

A reasonably specific description of the debtor's repayment obligations to the extent known by the creditor or creditor's representative.

# REAFFIRMATION AGREEMENT

P. 4

## 2. INSTRUCTIONS AND NOTICE TO DEBTOR

**Reaffirming a debt is a serious financial decision.** The law requires you to take certain steps to make sure the decision is in your best interest. If these steps are not completed, the reaffirmation agreement is not effective, even though you have signed it.

1. Read the disclosures in this Part A carefully. Consider the decision to reaffirm carefully. Then, if you want to reaffirm, sign the reaffirmation agreement in Part B (or you may use a separate agreement you and your creditor agree on).

2. Complete and sign Part D and be sure you can afford to make the payments you are agreeing to make and have received a copy of the disclosure statement and a completed and signed reaffirmation agreement.

3. If you were represented by an attorney during the negotiation of your reaffirmation agreement, the attorney must have signed the certification in Part C.

4. If you were not represented by an attorney during the negotiation of your reaffirmation agreement, you must have completed and signed Part E.

5. The original of this disclosure must be filed with the court by you or your creditor. If a separate reaffirmation agreement (other than the one in Part B) has been signed, it must be attached.

6. If the creditor is not a Credit Union and you were represented by an attorney during the negotiation of your reaffirmation agreement, your reaffirmation agreement becomes effective upon filing with the court unless the reaffirmation is presumed to be an undue hardship as explained in Part D. If the creditor is a Credit Union and you were represented by an attorney during the negotiation of your reaffirmation agreement, your reaffirmation agreement becomes effective upon filing with the court.

7. If you were not represented by an attorney during the negotiation of your reaffirmation agreement, it will not be effective unless the court approves it. The court will notify you and the creditor of the hearing on your reaffirmation agreement. You must attend this hearing in bankruptcy court where the judge will review your reaffirmation agreement. The bankruptcy court must approve your reaffirmation agreement as consistent with your best interests, except that no court approval is required if your reaffirmation agreement is for a consumer debt secured by a mortgage, deed of trust, security deed, or other lien on your real property, like your home.

P. 5

## YOUR RIGHT TO RESCIND (CANCEL) YOUR REAFFIRMATION AGREEMENT

You may rescind (cancel) your reaffirmation agreement at any time before the bankruptcy court enters a discharge order, or before the expiration of the 60-day period that begins on the date your reaffirmation agreement is filed with the court, whichever occurs later. To rescind (cancel) your reaffirmation agreement, you must notify the creditor that your reaffirmation agreement is rescinded (or canceled).

**Frequently Asked Questions:**

What are your obligations if you reaffirm the debt? A reaffirmed debt remains your personal legal obligation. It is not discharged in your bankruptcy case. That means that if you default on your reaffirmed debt after your bankruptcy case is over, your creditor may be able to take your property or your wages. Otherwise, your obligations will be determined by the reaffirmation agreement which may have changed the terms of the original agreement. For example, if you are reaffirming an open end credit agreement, the creditor may be permitted by that agreement or applicable law to change the terms of that agreement in the future under certain conditions.

Are you required to enter into a reaffirmation agreement by any law? No, you are not required to reaffirm a debt by any law. Only agree to reaffirm a debt if it is in your best interest. Be sure you can afford the payments you agree to make.

What if your creditor has a security interest or lien? Your bankruptcy discharge does not eliminate any lien on your property. A "lien" is often referred to as a security interest, deed of trust, mortgage or security deed. Even if you do not reaffirm and your personal liability on the debt is discharged, because of the lien your creditor may still have the right to take the security property if you do not pay the debt or default on it. If the lien is on an item of personal property that is exempt under your State's law or that the trustee has abandoned, you may be able to redeem the item rather than reaffirm the debt. To redeem, you make a single payment to the creditor equal to the current value of the security property, as agreed by the parties or determined by the court.

**NOTE:** When this disclosure refers to what a creditor "may" do, it does not use the word "may" to give the creditor specific permission. The word "may" is used to tell you what might occur if the law permits the creditor to take the action. If you have questions about your reaffirming a debt or what the law requires, consult with the attorney who helped you negotiate this agreement reaffirming a debt. If you don't have an attorney helping you, the judge will explain the effect of your reaffirming a debt when the hearing on the reaffirmation agreement is held.

REAFFIRMATION AGREEMENT

P. 6

**PART B: REAFFIRMATION AGREEMENT.**

I (we) agree to reaffirm the debts arising under the credit agreement described below.

1. Brief description of credit agreement:

2. Description of any changes to the credit agreement made as part of this reaffirmation agreement:

SIGNATURE(S):

| Borrower: | Co-borrower, if also reaffirming these debts: |

_____    _____
(Print Name)                   (Print Name)

_____    _____
(Signature)                    (Signature)
Date: _____          Date: _____

Accepted by creditor:

_____
(Print Name)

_____
(Signature)
Date of creditor acceptance: _____

# REAFFIRMATION AGREEMENT

P. 7

## PART C: CERTIFICATION BY DEBTOR'S ATTORNEY (IF ANY).

*[Check each applicable box.]*

☐ I hereby certify that (1) this agreement represents a fully informed and voluntary agreement by the debtor; (2) this agreement does not impose an undue hardship on the debtor or any dependent of the debtor; and (3) I have fully advised the debtor of the legal effect and consequences of this agreement and any default under this agreement.

☐ *[If applicable and the creditor is not a Credit Union.]* A presumption of undue hardship has been established with respect to this agreement. In my opinion, however, the debtor is able to make the required payment.

Printed Name of Debtor's Attorney: _____

Signature of Debtor's Attorney: _____

Date: _____

**REAFFIRMATION AGREEMENT**

P. 8

**PART D: DEBTOR'S STATEMENT IN SUPPORT OF REAFFIRMATION AGREEMENT**

*[Read and complete numbered paragraphs 1 and 2, OR, if the creditor is a Credit Union and the debtor is represented by an attorney, read the un-numbered paragraph below. Sign the appropriate signature line(s) and date your signature.]*

1. I believe this reaffirmation agreement will not impose an undue hardship on my dependents or me. I can afford to make the payments on the reaffirmed debt because my monthly income (take home pay plus any other income received) is $_____, and my actual current monthly expenses including monthly payments on post-bankruptcy debt and other reaffirmation agreements total $_____, leaving $_____ to make the required payments on this reaffirmed debt. I understand that if my income less my monthly expenses does not leave enough to make the payments, this reaffirmation agreement is presumed to be an undue hardship on me and must be reviewed by the court. However, this presumption may be overcome if I explain to the satisfaction of the court how I can afford to make the payments here: _____.

2. I received a copy of the Reaffirmation Disclosure Statement in Part A and a completed and signed reaffirmation agreement.

Signed: _____
    (Debtor)

_____
(Joint Debtor, if any)

Date: _____

— *Or*

*[If the creditor is a Credit Union and the debtor is represented by an attorney]*

I believe this reaffirmation agreement is in my financial interest. I can afford to make the payments on the reaffirmed debt. I received a copy of the Reaffirmation Disclosure Statement in Part A and a completed and signed reaffirmation agreement.

Signed: _____
    (Debtor)

_____
(Joint Debtor, if any)

Date: _____

P. 9

**PART E: MOTION FOR COURT APPROVAL**
*(To be completed only if the debtor is not represented by an attorney.)*

**MOTION FOR COURT APPROVAL OF REAFFIRMATION AGREEMENT**

I (we), the debtor(s), affirm the following to be true and correct:

I am not represented by an attorney in connection with this reaffirmation agreement.

I believe this reaffirmation agreement is in my best interest based on the income and expenses I have disclosed in my Statement in Support of this reaffirmation agreement, and because (provide any additional relevant reasons the court should consider):

Therefore, I ask the court for an order approving this reaffirmation agreement.

Signed:_____
       (Debtor)

_____
(Joint Debtor, if any)

Date: _____

**REAFFIRMATION AGREEMENT**

United States Bankruptcy Court
_____District of _____

In re _____,      Case No._____
                Debtor                                   Chapter _____

**ORDER APPROVING REAFFIRMATION AGREEMENT**

The debtor(s) _____ have filed a motion for approval of the
              (Name(s) of debtor(s))

reaffirmation agreement dated _____ made between the debtor(s) and
                             (Date of agreement)
_____. The court held the hearing required by 11 U.S.C. § 524(d)
     (Name of creditor)
on notice to the debtor(s) and the creditor on _____.
                                                       (Date)

COURT ORDER:    The court grants the debtor's motion and approves the reaffirmation agreement described above.

                                                                        BY THE COURT

Date: _____                       _____
                                                                     *United States Bankruptcy Judge*

# APPENDIX 20: BANKRUPTCY DISCHARGE ORDER

Form 18
(10/05)

## United States Bankruptcy Court

_____ District Of _____

In re _____, )
    *[Set forth here all names including married,*
    *maiden, and trade names used by debtor within*
    *last 8 years.]*
                       Debtor    ) Case No. _____

Address _____

_____ ) Chapter 7

Last four digits of Social Security No(s).: _____

Employer's Tax Identification No(s). *[if any]*: _____

**DISCHARGE OF DEBTOR**

It appearing that the debtor is entitled to a discharge, **IT IS ORDERED:** The debtor is granted a discharge under section 727 of title 11, United States Code, (the Bankruptcy Code).

Dated: _____

BY THE COURT

_____
United States Bankruptcy Judge

SEE THE BACK OF THIS ORDER FOR IMPORTANT INFORMATION.

## BANKRUPTCY DISCHARGE ORDER

Official Form 18 - Contd.
(10/05)

### EXPLANATION OF BANKRUPTCY DISCHARGE
### IN A CHAPTER 7 CASE

This court order grants a discharge to the person named as the debtor. It is not a dismissal of the case and it does not determine how much money, if any, the trustee will pay to creditors.

**Collection of Discharged Debts Prohibited**

The discharge prohibits any attempt to collect from the debtor a debt that has been discharged. For example, a creditor is not permitted to contact a debtor by mail, phone, or otherwise, to file or continue a lawsuit, to attach wages or other property, or to take any other action to collect a discharged debt from the debtor. *[In a case involving community property:* There are also special rules that protect certain community property owned by the debtor's spouse, even if that spouse did not file a bankruptcy case.] A creditor who violates this order can be required to pay damages and attorney's fees to the debtor.

However, a creditor may have the right to enforce a valid lien, such as a mortgage or security interest, against the debtor's property after the bankruptcy, if that lien was not avoided or eliminated in the bankruptcy case. Also, a debtor may voluntarily pay any debt that has been discharged.

**Debts That are Discharged**

The chapter 7 discharge order eliminates a debtor's legal obligation to pay a debt that is discharged. Most, but not all, types of debts are discharged if the debt existed on the date the bankruptcy case was filed. (If this case was begun under a different chapter of the Bankruptcy Code and converted to chapter 7, the discharge applies to debts owed when the bankruptcy case was converted.)

**Debts that are Not Discharged.**

Some of the common types of debts which are not discharged in a chapter 7 bankruptcy case are:

  a. Debts for most taxes;

  b. Debts incurred to pay nondischargeable taxes;

  c. Debts that are domestic support obligations;

  d. Debts for most student loans;

  e. Debts for most fines, penalties, forfeitures, or criminal restitution obligations;

  f. Debts for personal injuries or death caused by the debtor's operation of a motor vehicle, vessel, or aircraft while intoxicated;

  g. Some debts which were not properly listed by the debtor;

  h. Debts that the bankruptcy court specifically has decided or will decide in this bankruptcy case are not discharged;

  i. Debts for which the debtor has given up the discharge protections by signing a reaffirmation agreement in compliance with the Bankruptcy Code requirements for reaffirmation of debts.

  j. Debts owed to certain pension, profit sharing, stock bonus, other retirement plans, or to the Thrift Savings Plan for federal employees for certain types of loans from these plans.

This information is only a general summary of the bankruptcy discharge. There are exceptions to these general rules. Because the law is complicated, you may want to consult an attorney to determine the exact effect of the discharge in this case.

# APPENDIX 21: DIRECTORY OF UNITED STATES BANKRUPTCY COURTS MAIN OFFICES

| COURTHOUSE | ADDRESS | TELEPHONE | WEBSITE |
| --- | --- | --- | --- |
| Alabama Middle Bankruptcy Court | One Church Street Montgomery, AL 36104 | 334-954-3800 | www.almb.uscourts.gov |
| Alabama Northern Bankruptcy Court | 1800 Fifth Avenue North Birmingham, AL 35203 | 205-714-4002 | www.alnb.uscourts.gov |
| Alabama Southern Bankruptcy Court | 201 St. Louis Street Mobile, AL 36602 | 251-441-5391 | www.alsb.uscourts.gov |
| Alaska Bankruptcy Court | 605 West Fourth Avenue Anchorage, AK 99501 | 907-271-2655 | www.akb.uscourts.gov |
| Arizona Bankruptcy Court | 230 North First Avenue Phoenix, AZ 85003 | 602-682-4000 | www.azb.uscourts.gov |
| Arkansas Eastern & Western Bankruptcy Court | 300 West Second Street Little Rock AR 72201 | 501-918-5500 | www.areb.uscourts.gov |
| California Central Bankruptcy Court | 255 East Temple Street Los Angeles, CA 90012 | 213-894-3118 | www.cacb.uscourts.gov |
| California Eastern Bankruptcy Court | 501 I Street Sacramento, CA 95814 | 916-930-4400 | www.caeb.uscourts.gov |
| California Northern Bankruptcy Court | 235 Pine Street San Francisco, CA 94104 | 415-268-2300 | www.canb.uscourts.gov |

# DIRECTORY OF UNITED STATES BANKRUPTCY COURTS MAIN OFFICES

| | | | |
|---|---|---|---|
| California Southern Bankruptcy Court | 325 West F Street San Diego, CA 92101 | 619-557-5620 | www.casb.uscourts.gov |
| Colorado Bankruptcy Court | 721 19th Street Denver, CO 80202 | 303-844-4045 | www.cob.uscourts.gov |
| Connecticut Bankruptcy Court | 450 Main Street Hartford, CT 06103 | 860-240-3675 | www.ctb.uscourts.gov |
| Delaware Bankruptcy Court | 824 North Market Street Wilmington, DE 19801 | 302-252-2900 | www.deb.uscourts.gov |
| District of Columbia Bankruptcy Court | 333 Constitution Avenue N.W. Washington, DC 20001 | 202-565-2500 | www.dcb.uscourts.gov |
| Florida Middle Bankruptcy Court | 801 North Florida Avenue Tampa, FL 33602 | 813-301-5162 | www.flmb.uscourts.gov |
| Florida Northern Bankruptcy Court | 110 East Park Avenue Tallahassee, FL 32301 | 850-521-5001 | www.flnb.uscourts.gov |
| Florida Southern Bankruptcy Court | 51 Southwest First Avenue Miami, FL 33130 | 305-714-1800 | www.flsb.uscourts.gov |
| Georgia Middle Bankruptcy Court | 433 Cherry Street Macon, GA 31201 | 478-752-3506 | www.gamb.uscourts.gov |
| Georgia Northern Bankruptcy Court | 75 Spring Street SW Atlanta, GA 30303 | 404-215-1000 | www.ganb.uscourts.gov |
| Georgia Southern Bankruptcy Court | 125 Bull Street Savannah, GA 31402 | 912-650-4100 | www.gasb.uscourts.gov |
| Hawaii Bankruptcy Court | 1132 Bishop Street Honolulu, HHI 96813 | 808-522-8100 | www.hib.uscourts.gov |
| Idaho Bankruptcy Court | 550 West Fort Street Boise, ID 83724 | 208-334-1361 | www.id.uscourts.gov |
| Illinois Central Bankruptcy Court | 600 East Monroe Street Springfield, IL 62701 | 217-492-4551 | www.ilcb.uscourts.gov |
| Illinois Northern Bankruptcy Court | 219 South Dearborn Street Chicago, IL 60604 | 312-435-5694 | www.ilnb.uscourts.gov |

## DIRECTORY OF UNITED STATES BANKRUPTCY COURTS MAIN OFFICES

| | | | |
|---|---|---|---|
| Illinois Southern Bankruptcy Court | 750 Missouri Avenue East St. Louis, IL 62201 | 618-482-9400 | www.ilsb.uscourts.gov |
| Indiana Northern Bankruptcy Court | 401 South Michigan Street South Bend, IN 46601 | 574-968-2100 | www.innb.uscourts.gov |
| Indiana Southern Bankruptcy Court | 46 East Ohio Street Indianapolis, IN 46204 | 317-229-3800 | www.insb.uscourts.gov |
| Iowa Northern Bankruptcy Court | 425 Second Street Southeast Cedar Rapids, IA 52401 | 319-286-2200 | www.ianb.uscourts.gov |
| Iowa Southern Bankruptcy Court | 110 East Court Avenue Des Moines, IA 50309 | 515-284-6230 | www.iasb.uscourts.gov |
| Kansas Bankruptcy Court | 401 North Market Street Wichita, KS 67202 | 316-269-6486 | www.ksb.uscourts.gov |
| Kentucky Eastern Bankruptcy Court | 100 East Vine Street Lexington, KY 40507 | 859-233-2608 | www.kyeb.uscourts.gov |
| Kentucky Western Bankruptcy Court | 601 West Broadway Louisville, KY 40202 | 502-627-5800 | www.kywb.uscourts.gov |
| Louisiana Eastern Bankruptcy Court | 500 Poydras Street New Orleans, LA 70130 | 504-589-7878 | www.laeb.uscourts.gov |
| Louisiana Middle Bankruptcy Court | 707 Florida Street Baton Rouge, LA 70801 | 225-389-0211 | www.lamb.uscourts.gov |
| Louisiana Western Bankruptcy Court | 300 Fannin Street Shreveport, LA 71101 | 318-676-4267 | www.lawb.uscourts.gov |
| Maine Bankruptcy Court | 537 Congress Street Portland, ME 04101-3306 | 207-780-3482 | www.meb.uscourts.gov |
| Maryland Bankruptcy Court | 101 West Lombard Street Baltimore, MD 21201 | 410-962-2688 | www.mdb.uscourts.gov |
| Massachusetts Bankruptcy Court | 10 Causeway Street Boston, MA 02222 | 617-565-8950 | www.mab.uscourts.gov |

# DIRECTORY OF UNITED STATES BANKRUPTCY COURTS MAIN OFFICES

| | | | |
|---|---|---|---|
| Michigan Eastern Bankruptcy Court | 211 West Fort Street Detroit, MI 48226 | 313-234-0068 | www.mieb.uscourts.gov |
| Michigan Western Bankruptcy Court | One Division Street NW Grand Rapids, MI 49503 | 616-456-2693 | www.miwb.uscourts.gov |
| Minnesota Bankruptcy Court | 300 South Fourth Street Minneapolis, MN 55415 | 612-664-5200 | www.mnb.uscourts.gov |
| Mississippi Northern Bankruptcy Court | 703 Highway 145 North Aberdeen, MS 39730 | 662-369-2596 | www.msnb.uscourts.gov |
| Mississippi Southern Bankruptcy Court | 100 East Capitol Street Jackson, MS 39201 | 601-965-5301 | www.mssb.uscourts.gov |
| Missouri Eastern Bankruptcy Court | 111 South Tenth Street St. Louis, MO 63102 | 314-244-4500 | www.moeb.uscourts.gov |
| Missouri Western Bankruptcy Court | 400 East Ninth Street, Kansas City, MO 64106 | 816-512-5000 | www.mow.uscourts.gov |
| Montana Bankruptcy Court | 400 North Main Street Butte, MT 59701 | 406-782-3354 | www.mtb.uscourts.gov |
| Nebraska Bankruptcy Court | 111 South 18th Plaza Omaha, NE 68102 | 402-661-7444 | www.neb.uscourts.gov |
| Nevada Bankruptcy Court | 300 Las Vegas Boulevard South Las Vegas, NV 89101 | 702-388-6257 | www.nvb.uscourts.gov |
| New Hampshire Bankruptcy Court | 1000 Elm Street Manchester, NH 03101 | 603-222-2600 | www.nhb.uscourts.gov |
| New Jersey Bankruptcy Court | 50 Walnut Street Newark, NJ 07102 | 973-645-4764 | www.njb.uscourts.gov |
| New Mexico Bankruptcy Court | 500 Gold Avenue SW Albuquerque, NM 87102 | 505-348-2500 | www.nmcourt.fed.us |
| New York Eastern Bankruptcy Court | 271 Cadman Plaza East Brooklyn, NY 11201 | 347-394-1700 | www.nyeb.uscourts.gov |

## DIRECTORY OF UNITED STATES BANKRUPTCY COURTS MAIN OFFICES

| | | | |
|---|---|---|---|
| New York Northern Bankruptcy Court | 445 Broadway Albany, NY 12207 | 518-257-1661 | www.nynb.uscourts.gov |
| New York Southern Bankruptcy Court | One Bowling Green New York NY 10004 | 212-668-2870 | www.nysb.uscourts.gov |
| New York Western Bankruptcy Court | 100 State Street Rochester, NY 14614 | 585-613-4200 | www.nywb.uscourts.gov |
| North Carolina Eastern Bankruptcy Court | 1760 Parkwood Boulevard West Wilson, NC 27893 | 252-237-0248 | www.nceb.uscourts.gov |
| North Carolina Middle Bankruptcy Court | 101 South Edgeworth Street Greensboro, NC 27401 | 336-333-5647 | www.ncmb.uscourts.gov |
| North Carolina Western Bankruptcy Court | 401 West Trade Street Charlotte, NC 28202 | 704-350-7500 | www.ncwb.uscourts.gov |
| North Dakota Bankruptcy Court | 655 First Avenue North Fargo, ND 58102 | 701-297-7100 | www.ndb.uscourts.gov |
| Ohio Northern Bankruptcy Court | 201 Superior Avenue, Cleveland, OH 44114 | 216-615-4300 | www.ohnb.uscourts.gov |
| Ohio Southern Bankruptcy Court | 120 West Third Street Dayton, OH 45402 | 937-225-2516 | www.ohsb.uscourts.gov |
| Oklahoma Eastern Bankruptcy Court | 111 West Fourth Street Okmulgee, OK 74447 | 918-758-0126 | www.okeb.uscourts.gov |
| Oklahoma Northern Bankruptcy Court | 224 South Boulder Avenue Tulsa, OK 74103 | 918-699-4000 | www.oknb.uscourts.gov |
| Oklahoma Western Bankruptcy Court | 215 Dean A. McGee Avenue Oklahoma City, OK 73102 | 405-609-5700 | www.okwb.uscourts.gov |
| Oregon Bankruptcy Court | 1001 Southwest Fifth Avenue Portland, OR 97204 | 503-326-2231 | www.orb.uscourts.gov |
| Pennsylvania Eastern Bankruptcy Court | 900 Market Street Philadelphia, PA 19107 | 215-408-2800 | www.paeb.uscourts.gov |

# DIRECTORY OF UNITED STATES BANKRUPTCY COURTS MAIN OFFICES

| | | | |
|---|---|---|---|
| Pennsylvania Middle Bankruptcy Court | 197 South Main Street Wilkes Barre, PA 18701 | 570-826-6450 | www.pamb.uscourts.gov |
| Pennsylvania Western Bankruptcy Court | 600 Grant Street Pittsburgh, PA 15219 | 412-644-4060 | www.pawb.uscourts.gov |
| Puerto Rico Bankruptcy Court | 300 Calle Del Recinto Sur San Juan, PR 00901 | 787-977-6000 | www.prb.uscourts.gov |
| Rhode Island Bankruptcy Court | 380 Westminster Mall Providence, RI 02903 | 401-528-4477 | www.rib.uscourts.gov |
| South Carolina Bankruptcy Court | 1100 Laurel Street Columbia, SC 29201 | 803-765-5436 | www.scb.uscourts.gov |
| South Dakota Bankruptcy Court | 400 South Phillips Avenue Sioux Falls, SD 57104 | 605-330-4541 | www.sdb.uscourts.gov |
| Tennessee Eastern Bankruptcy Court | 31 East 11th Street Chattanooga, TN 37402 | 423-752-5163 | www.tneb.uscourts.gov |
| Tennessee Middle Bankruptcy Court | 701 Broadway Nashville, TN 37203 | 615-736-5590 | www.tnmb.uscourts.gov |
| Tennessee Western Bankruptcy Court | 200 Jefferson Avenue Memphis, TN 38103 | 901-328-3500 | www.tnwb.uscourts.gov |
| Texas Eastern Bankruptcy Court | 110 North College Avenue Tyler, TX 75702 | 903-590-3200 | www.txeb.uscourts.gov |
| Texas Northern Bankruptcy Court | 1100 Commerce Street Dallas, TX 75242 | 214-753-2000 | www.tnxb.uscourts.gov |
| Texas Southern Bankruptcy Court | 515 Rusk Street Houston, TX 77002 | 713-250-5500 | www.txsb.uscourts.gov |
| Texas Western Bankruptcy Court | 615 East Houston Street San Antonio, TX 78205 | 210-472-5187 | www.txwb.uscourts.gov |
| Utah Bankruptcy Court | 350 South Main Street Salt Lake City, UT 84101 | 801-524-6687 | www.utb.uscourts.gov |
| Vermont Bankruptcy Court | 67 Merchants Row Rutland, VT 05701 | 802-776-2000 | www.vtb.uscourts.gov |

| | | | |
|---|---|---|---|
| Virginia Eastern Bankruptcy Court | 1100 East Main Street Richmond, VA 23219 | 804-916-2400 | www.vaeb.uscourts.gov |
| Virginia Western Bankruptcy Court | 210 Church Avenue SW Roanoke, VA 24011 | 540-857-2391 | www.vawb.uscourts.gov |
| Washington Eastern Bankruptcy Court | 904 West Riverside Avenue Spokane, WA 99201 | 509-353-2404 | www.waeb.uscourts.gov |
| Washington Western Bankruptcy Court | 700 Stewart Street Seattle, WA 98101 | 206-370-5200 | www.wawb.uscourts.gov |
| West Virginia Northern Bankruptcy Court | 1125 Chapline Street Wheeling, WV 26003 | 304-233-1655 | www.wvnb.uscourts.gov |
| West Virginia Southern Bankruptcy Court | 300 Virginia Street East Charleston, WV 25301 | 304-347-3003 | www.wvsb.uscourts.gov |
| Wisconsin Eastern Bankruptcy Court | 517 East Wisconsin Avenue Milwaukee, WI 53202 | 414-297-3291 | www.wieb.uscourts.gov |

Source: Administrative Office of the U.S. Courts

# APPENDIX 22: DISCLOSURE FEES UNDER THE FAIR AND ACCURATE CREDIT TRANSACTIONS (FACT) ACT

**SECTION 1681J. CHARGES FOR CERTAIN DISCLOSURES**

(a) Free annual disclosure

(1) Nationwide consumer reporting agencies

(A) In general

All consumer reporting agencies described in subsections (p) and (w) of section 1681a of this title shall make all disclosures pursuant to section 1681g of this title once during any 12-month period upon request of the consumer and without charge to the consumer.

(B) Centralized source

Subparagraph (A) shall apply with respect to a consumer reporting agency described in section 1681a(p) of this title only if the request from the consumer is made using the centralized source established for such purpose in accordance with section 211(c) of the Fair and Accurate Credit Transactions Act of 2003.

(C) Nationwide specialty consumer reporting agency

(i) In general

The Commission shall prescribe regulations applicable to each consumer reporting agency described in section 1681a (w) of this title to require the establishment of a streamlined process for consumers to request consumer reports under subparagraph (A), which shall include, at a minimum, the establishment by each such agency of a toll-free telephone number for such requests.

(ii) Considerations

In prescribing regulations under clause (i), the Commission shall consider—

(I) the significant demands that may be placed on consumer reporting agencies in providing such consumer reports;

(II) appropriate means to ensure that consumer reporting agencies can satisfactorily meet those demands, including the efficacy of a system of staggering the availability to consumers of such consumer reports; and

(III) the ease by which consumers should be able to contact consumer reporting agencies with respect to access to such consumer reports.

(iii) Date of issuance

The Commission shall issue the regulations required by this subparagraph in final form not later than 6 months after December 4, 2003.

(iv) Consideration of ability to comply

The regulations of the Commission under this subparagraph shall establish an effective date by which each nationwide specialty consumer reporting agency (as defined in section 1681a(w) of this title) shall be required to comply with subsection (a) of this section, which effective date—

(I) shall be established after consideration of the ability of each nationwide specialty consumer reporting agency to comply with subsection (a) of this section; and

(II) shall be not later than 6 months after the date on which such regulations are issued in final form (or such additional period not to exceed 3 months, as the Commission determines appropriate).

(2) Timing

A consumer reporting agency shall provide a consumer report under paragraph (1) not later than 15 days after the date on which the request is received under paragraph (1).

(3) Reinvestigations

Notwithstanding the time periods specified in section 1681i(a)(1) of this title, a reinvestigation under that section by a consumer reporting agency upon a request of a consumer that is made after receiving a consumer report under this subsection shall be completed not later than 45 days after the date on which the request is received.

(4) Exception for first 12 months of operation

This subsection shall not apply to a consumer reporting agency that has not been furnishing consumer reports to third parties on a continuing basis during the 12-month period preceding a request under paragraph (1), with respect to consumers residing nationwide.

(b) Free disclosure after adverse notice to consumer

Each consumer reporting agency that maintains a file on a consumer shall make all disclosures pursuant to section 1681g of this title without charge to the consumer if, not later than 60 days after receipt by such consumer of a notification pursuant to section 1681m of this title, or of a notification from a debt collection agency affiliated with that consumer reporting agency stating that the consumer's credit rating may be or has been adversely affected, the consumer makes a request under section 1681g of this title.

(c) Free disclosure under certain other circumstances

Upon the request of the consumer, a consumer reporting agency shall make all disclosures pursuant to section 1681g of this title once during any 12-month period without charge to that consumer if the consumer certifies in writing that the consumer—

(1) is unemployed and intends to apply for employment in the 60-day period beginning on the date on which the certification is made;

(2) is a recipient of public welfare assistance; or

(3) has reason to believe that the file on the consumer at the agency contains inaccurate information due to fraud.

(d) Free disclosures in connection with fraud alerts

Upon the request of a consumer, a consumer reporting agency described in section 1681a(p) of this title shall make all disclosures pursuant to section 1681g of this title without charge to the consumer, as provided in subsections (a)(2) and (b)(2) of section 1681c-1 of this title, as applicable.

(e) Other charges prohibited

A consumer reporting agency shall not impose any charge on a consumer for providing any notification required by this subchapter or making any disclosure required by this subchapter, except as authorized by subsection (f) of this section.

(f) Reasonable charges allowed for certain disclosures

(1) In general

In the case of a request from a consumer other than a request that is covered by any of subsections (a) through (d) of this section, a consumer reporting agency may impose a reasonable charge on a consumer—

(A) for making a disclosure to the consumer pursuant to section 1681g of this title, which charge

(i) shall not exceed $8; and

(ii) shall be indicated to the consumer before making the disclosure; and

(B) for furnishing, pursuant to section 1681i(d) of this title, following a reinvestigation under section 1681i(a) of this title, a statement, codification, or summary to a person designated by the consumer under that section after the 30-day period beginning on the date of notification of the consumer under paragraph (6) or (8) of section 1681i(a) of this title with respect to the reinvestigation, which charge -

(i) shall not exceed the charge that the agency would impose on each designated recipient for a consumer report; and

(ii) shall be indicated to the consumer before furnishing such information.

(2) Modification of amount

The Federal Trade Commission shall increase the amount referred to in paragraph (1)(A)(i) on January 1 of each year, based proportionally on changes in the Consumer Price Index, with fractional changes rounded to the nearest fifty cents; then only to the extent of the inconsistency.

# APPENDIX 23: CREDIT REPORTING AGENCY INFORMATION DISPUTE LETTER

[Name of Credit Reporting Agency]

[Address]

[City, State, Zip Code]

Attn: Complaint Department

Dear Sir or Madam:

I am writing to dispute the following information contained in my credit file with your Company. The items I dispute are also encircled on the attached copy of the credit report I received from your office, as follows:

*Item #1*: (Identify item(s) disputed by name of source, such as creditors or tax court, and identify type of item, such as credit account, judgment, etc.) This item is (inaccurate or incomplete) because (describe what is inaccurate or incomplete and why). I am requesting that the item be deleted (or request another specific change) to correct the information. Enclosed are copies of (use this sentence if applicable and describe any enclosed documentation, such as payment records, court documents) supporting my position.

*Item #2*: Same as above for any additional disputed information.

Please reinvestigate this (these) matter(s) and (delete or correct) the disputed item(s) as soon as possible.

Sincerely,

John Doe

Enclosures: (List what you are enclosing)

# APPENDIX 24: CREDIT REPORT CHECKLIST

## TRUECREDIT CREDIT REPORT CHECKLIST

You can't erase the past, but you can definitely work on improving the future. Improving your credit and boosting your score is doable with a little hard work and a little help from TrueCredit. The following checklist will help you get started - just print out this worksheet each time you check your credit report and file away the copies so you can track your improvement over time.

### STEP 1: GET THE FACTS

Order your 3-in-1 Credit Report and 3 Credit Scores online. Check that the following information is correct on each report:

**Date of Credit Check:** _____

**Equifax:**

____ Name
____ Birth Date
____ Address
____ Employer
____ Consumer Statement
____ Number of Accounts
____ Account Types
____ Account Status
____ Account Dates
____ Account Limits
____ Payment History
____ Collection Accounts
____ Public Records
____ Inquiries

**Credit Score:** _____

**Dealing with Debt**

# CREDIT REPORT CHECKLIST

**TransUnion:**

\_\_\_\_ Name
\_\_\_\_ Birth Date
\_\_\_\_ Address
\_\_\_\_ Employer
\_\_\_\_ Consumer Statement
\_\_\_\_ Number of Accounts
\_\_\_\_ Account Types
\_\_\_\_ Account Status
\_\_\_\_ Account Dates
\_\_\_\_ Account Limits
\_\_\_\_ Payment History
\_\_\_\_ Collection Accounts
\_\_\_\_ Public Records
\_\_\_\_ Inquiries

**Credit Score:** _____

**Experian:**

\_\_\_\_ Name
\_\_\_\_ Birth Date
\_\_\_\_ Address
\_\_\_\_ Employer
\_\_\_\_ Consumer Statement
\_\_\_\_ Number of Accounts
\_\_\_\_ Account Types
\_\_\_\_ Account Status
\_\_\_\_ Account Dates
\_\_\_\_ Account Limits
\_\_\_\_ Payment History
\_\_\_\_ Collection Accounts
\_\_\_\_ Public Records
\_\_\_\_ Inquiries

**Credit Score:** _____

# CREDIT REPORT CHECKLIST

## STEP 2: MAINTAIN ACCURACY

Should you find an inaccuracy, contact the creditor responsible for the account first to make the update. If this doesn't work, contact the credit reporting agencies to dispute the record. Log your actions here -

**EXAMPLE:**

**Issue:** Example – Inaccurate Late Payment

**Action:** Called creditor to investigate

**Result:** Creditor updated account

**Issue:**

**Action:**

**Result:**

**Issue:**

**Action:**

**Result:**

**Issue:**

**Action:**

**Result:**

Dealing with Debt

# CREDIT REPORT CHECKLIST

## STEP 3: IMPROVE YOUR BEHAVIOR

Make a plan to improve your credit behavior. If you have trouble making payments, sign up for an automated service. If you have too much debt, make a plan for improvement. Record your goals here -

**EXAMPLE:**

**Issue:**   Too much debt

**Action:**   I will pay $400 a month to reduce it

**Result:**   I can pay off the debt in 10 months


**Issue:**

**Action:**

**Result:**


**Issue:**

**Action:**

**Result:**


**Issue:**

**Action:**

**Result:**

## CREDIT REPORT CHECKLIST

**STEP 4: FOLLOW-UP**

Check your credit reports again in 30-60 days to see how your credit has improved. Print out a new copy of this checklist and run through these steps again. Keep copies of these worksheets to document your progress over time. Your credit goals are within your reach!

**STEP 5: MONITOR YOUR CREDIT**

To guard against fraud and keep your credit healthy, sign up for a Credit Monitoring service that will quickly alert you to any changes in your report. TrueCredit's ID Fraud-Watch™ combines weekly credit alert emails, four credit reports a year and $25,000 Identity Theft Insurance.

# APPENDIX 25:
# THE CREDIT REPAIR ORGANIZATIONS ACT

**15 U.S.C. § 1679. FINDINGS AND PURPOSES.**

(a) Findings.—The Congress makes the following findings:

(1) Consumers have a vital interest in establishing and maintaining their credit worthiness and credit standing in order to obtain and use credit. As a result, consumers who have experienced credit problems may seek assistance from credit repair organizations which offer to improve the credit standing of such consumers.

(2) Certain advertising and business practices of some companies engaged in the business of credit repair services have worked a financial hardship upon consumers, particularly those of limited economic means and who are inexperienced in credit matters.

(b) Purposes.—The purposes of this title are—

(1) to ensure that prospective buyers of the services of credit repair organizations are provided with the information necessary to make an informed decision regarding the purchase of such services; and

(2) to protect the public from unfair or deceptive advertising and business practices by credit repair organizations.

**SECTION 1679A. DEFINITIONS.**

For purposes of this subchapter, the following definitions apply:

(1) Consumer.—The term 'consumer' means an individual.

(2) Consumer credit transaction.—The term 'consumer credit transaction' means any transaction in which credit is offered or extended to an individual for personal, family, or household purposes.

(3) Credit repair organization.—The term 'credit repair organization'—

(A) means any person who uses any instrumentality of interstate commerce or the mails to sell, provide, or perform (or represent that such person can or will sell, provide, or perform) any service, in return for the payment of money or other valuable consideration, for the express or implied purpose of—

(i) improving any consumer's credit record, credit history, or credit rating; or

(ii) providing advice or assistance to any consumer with regard to any activity or service described in clause (i); and

(B) does not include—

(i) any nonprofit organization which is exempt from taxation under section 501(c)(3) of title 26;

(ii) any creditor (as defined in section 1602 of this title), with respect to any consumer, to the extent the creditor is assisting the consumer to restructure any debt owed by the consumer to the creditor; or

(iii) any depository institution (as that term is defined in section 1813 of title 12) or any Federal or State credit union (as those terms are defined in section 1752 of title 12), or any affiliate or subsidiary of such a depository institution or credit union.

(4) Credit.—The term 'credit' has the meaning given to such term in section 1602(e) of this title.

### SECTION 1679B. PROHIBITED PRACTICES.

(a) In General.—No person may—

(1) make any statement, or counsel or advise any consumer to make any statement, which is untrue or misleading (or which, upon the exercise of reasonable care, should be known by the credit repair organization, officer, employee, agent, or other person to be untrue or misleading) with respect to any consumer's credit worthiness, credit standing, or credit capacity to—

(A) any consumer reporting agency (as defined in section 1681a (f) of this title); or

(B) any person—

(i) who has extended credit to the consumer; or

(ii) to whom the consumer has applied or is applying for an extension of credit;

(2) make any statement, or counsel or advise any consumer to make any statement, the intended effect of which is to alter the consumer's identification to prevent the display of the consumer's credit record, history, or rating for the purpose of concealing adverse information that is accurate and not obsolete to—

(A) any consumer reporting agency;

(B) any person—

(i) who has extended credit to the consumer; or

(ii) to whom the consumer has applied or is applying for an extension of credit;

(3) make or use any untrue or misleading representation of the services of the credit repair organization; or

(4) engage, directly or indirectly, in any act, practice, or course of business that constitutes or results in the commission of, or an attempt to commit, a fraud or deception on any person in connection with the offer or sale of the services of the credit repair organization.

(b) Payment in Advance.—No credit repair organization may charge or receive any money or other valuable consideration for the performance of any service which the credit repair organization has agreed to perform for any consumer before such service is fully performed.

### SECTION 1679C. DISCLOSURES.

(a) Disclosure Required.—Any credit repair organization shall provide any consumer with the following written statement before any contract or agreement between the consumer and the credit repair organization is executed:

#### CONSUMER CREDIT FILE RIGHTS UNDER STATE AND FEDERAL LAW

You have a right to dispute inaccurate information in your credit report by contacting the credit bureau directly. However, neither you nor any "credit repair" company or credit repair organization has the right to have accurate, current, and verifiable information removed from your credit report. The credit bureau must remove accurate, negative information from your report only if it is over 7 years old. Bankruptcy information can be reported for 10 years.

You have a right to obtain a copy of your credit report from a credit bureau. You may be charged a reasonable fee. There is no fee, however, if you have been turned down for credit, employment, insurance, or a rental dwelling because of information in your credit report within the preceding 60 days. The credit bureau must provide

## THE CREDIT REPAIR ORGANIZATIONS ACT

someone to help you interpret the information in your credit file. You are entitled to receive a free copy of your credit report if you are unemployed and intend to apply for employment in the next 60 days, if you are a recipient of public welfare assistance, or if you have reason to believe that there is inaccurate information in your credit report due to fraud.

You have a right to sue a credit repair organization that violates the Credit Repair Organization Act. This law prohibits deceptive practices by credit repair organizations.

You have the right to cancel your contract with any credit repair organization for any reason within 3 business days from the date you signed it.

Credit bureaus are required to follow reasonable procedures to ensure that the information they report is accurate. However, mistakes may occur.

You may, on your own, notify a credit bureau in writing that you dispute the accuracy of information in your credit file. The credit bureau must then reinvestigate and modify or remove inaccurate or incomplete information. The credit bureau may not charge any fee for this service. Any pertinent information and copies of all documents you have concerning an error should be given to the credit bureau.

If the credit bureau's reinvestigation does not resolve the dispute to your satisfaction, you may send a brief statement to the credit bureau, to be kept in your file, explaining why you think the record is inaccurate. The credit bureau must include a summary of your statement about disputed information with any report it issues about you.

The Federal Trade Commission regulates credit bureaus and credit repair organizations. For more information contact:

> The Public Reference Branch
> Federal Trade Commission
> Washington, D.C. 20580'.

(b) Separate Statement Requirement.—The written statement required under this section shall be provided as a document which is separate from any written contract or other agreement between the credit repair organization and the consumer or any other written material provided to the consumer.

(c) Retention of Compliance Records.—

(1) In general.—The credit repair organization shall maintain a copy of the statement signed by the consumer acknowledging receipt of the statement.

(2) Maintenance for 2 years.—The copy of any consumer's statement shall be maintained in the organization's files for 2 years after the date on which the statement is signed by the consumer.

### SECTION 1679D. CREDIT REPAIR ORGANIZATIONS CONTRACTS.

(a) Written Contracts Required.—No services may be provided by any credit repair organization for any consumer—

(1) unless a written and dated contract (for the purchase of such services) which meets the requirements of subsection (b) has been signed by the consumer; or

(2) before the end of the 3-business-day period beginning on the date the contract is signed.

(b) Terms and Conditions of Contract.—No contract referred to in subsection (a) meets the requirements of this subsection unless such contract includes (in writing)—

(1) the terms and conditions of payment, including the total amount of all payments to be made by the consumer to the credit repair organization or to any other person;

(2) a full and detailed description of the services to be performed by the credit repair organization for the consumer, including—

(A) all guarantees of performance; and

(B) an estimate of—

(i) the date by which the performance of the services (to be performed by the credit repair organization or any other person) will be complete; or

(ii) the length of the period necessary to perform such services;

(3) the credit repair organization's name and principal business address; and

(4) a conspicuous statement in bold face type, in immediate proximity to the space reserved for the consumer's signature on the contract, which reads as follows: 'You may cancel this contract without penalty or obligation at any time before midnight of the 3rd business day after the date on which you signed the contract. See the attached notice of cancellation form for an explanation of this right.'.

## THE CREDIT REPAIR ORGANIZATIONS ACT

### SECTION 1679E. RIGHT TO CANCEL CONTRACT.

(a) In General.—Any consumer may cancel any contract with any credit repair organization without penalty or obligation by notifying the credit repair organization of the consumer's intention to do so at any time before midnight of the 3rd business day which begins after the date on which the contract or agreement between the consumer and the credit repair organization is executed or would, but for this subsection, become enforceable against the parties.

(b) Cancellation Form and Other Information.—Each contract shall be accompanied by a form, in duplicate, which has the heading 'Notice of Cancellation' and contains in bold face type the following statement:

> 'You may cancel this contract, without any penalty or obligation, at any time before midnight of the 3rd day which begins after the date the contract is signed by you.
>
> To cancel this contract, mail or deliver a signed, dated copy of this cancellation notice, or any other written notice to (name of credit repair organization) at (address of credit repair organization) before midnight on (date).
>
> I hereby cancel this transaction,
>
> (date)
>
> (purchaser's signature).'.

(c) Consumer Copy of Contract Required.—Any consumer who enters into any contract with any credit repair organization shall be given, by the organization—

> (1) a copy of the completed contract and the disclosure statement required under section 1679c of this title; and
>
> (2) a copy of any other document the credit repair organization requires the consumer to sign, at the time the contract or the other document is signed.

### SECTION 1679F. NONCOMPLIANCE WITH THIS TITLE.

(a) Consumer Waivers Invalid.—Any waiver by any consumer of any protection provided by or any right of the consumer under this title—

> (1) shall be treated as void; and
>
> (2) may not be enforced by any Federal or State court or any other person.

(b) Attempt To Obtain Waiver.—Any attempt by any person to obtain a waiver from any consumer of any protection provided by or any right of the consumer under this title shall be treated as a violation of this title.

(c) Contracts Not in Compliance.—Any contract for services which does not comply with the applicable provisions of this title—

(1) shall be treated as void; and

(2) may not be enforced by any Federal or State court or any other person.

**1679G. CIVIL LIABILITY.**

(a) Liability Established.—Any person who fails to comply with any provision of this title with respect to any other person shall be liable to such person in an amount equal to the sum of the amounts determined under each of the following paragraphs:

(1) Actual damages.—The greater of—

(A) the amount of any actual damage sustained by such person as a result of such failure; or

(B) any amount paid by the person to the credit repair organization.

(2) Punitive damages.—

(A) Individual actions.—In the case of any action by an individual, such additional amount as the court may allow.

(B) Class actions.—In the case of a class action, the sum of—

(i) the aggregate of the amount which the court may allow for each named plaintiff; and

(ii) the aggregate of the amount which the court may allow for each other class member, without regard to any minimum individual recovery.

(3) Attorneys' fees.—In the case of any successful action to enforce any liability under paragraph (1) or (2), the costs of the action, together with reasonable attorneys' fees.

(b) Factors to Be Considered in Awarding Punitive Damages.—In determining the amount of any liability of any credit repair organization under subsection (a)(2), the court shall consider, among other relevant factors—

(1) the frequency and persistence of noncompliance by the credit repair organization;

(2) the nature of the noncompliance;

(3) the extent to which such noncompliance was intentional; and

(4) in the case of any class action, the number of consumers adversely affected.

### SECTION 1679H. ADMINISTRATIVE ENFORCEMENT.

(a) In General.—Compliance with the requirements imposed under this title with respect to credit repair organizations shall be enforced under the Federal Trade Commission Act [15 U.S.C. 41 et seq.] by the Federal Trade Commission.

(b) Violations of This Title Treated as Violations of Federal Trade Commission Act.—

(1) In general.—For the purpose of the exercise by the Federal Trade Commission of the Commission's functions and powers under the Federal Trade Commission Act [15 U.S.C. 41 et seq.], any violation of any requirement or prohibition imposed under this subchapter with respect to credit repair organizations shall constitute an unfair or deceptive act or practice in commerce in violation of section 5(a) of the Federal Trade Commission Act [15 U.S.C. 45 (a)].

(2) Enforcement authority under other law.—All functions and powers of the Federal Trade Commission under the Federal Trade Commission Act shall be available to the Commission to enforce compliance with this title by any person subject to enforcement by the Federal Trade Commission pursuant to this subsection, including the power to enforce the provisions of this title in the same manner as if the violation had been a violation of any Federal Trade Commission trade regulation rule, without regard to whether the credit repair organization—

(A) is engaged in commerce; or

(B) meets any other jurisdictional tests in the Federal Trade Commission Act.

(c) State Action for Violations.—

(1) Authority of states.—In addition to such other remedies as are provided under State law, whenever the chief law enforcement officer of a State, or an official or agency designated by a State, has reason to believe that any person has violated or is violating this title, the State—

(A) may bring an action to enjoin such violation;

## THE CREDIT REPAIR ORGANIZATIONS ACT

(B) may bring an action on behalf of its residents to recover damages for which the person is liable to such residents under section 1679g of this title as a result of the violation; and

(C) in the case of any successful action under subparagraph (A) or (B), shall be awarded the costs of the action and reasonable attorney fees as determined by the court.

(2) Rights of commission.—

(A) Notice to commission.—The State shall serve prior written notice of any civil action under paragraph (1) upon the Federal Trade Commission and provide the Commission with a copy of its complaint, except in any case where such prior notice is not feasible, in which case the State shall serve such notice immediately upon instituting such action.

(B) Intervention.—The Commission shall have the right—

(i) to intervene in any action referred to in subparagraph (A);

(ii) upon so intervening, to be heard on all matters arising in the action; and

(iii) to file petitions for appeal.

(3) Investigatory powers.—For purposes of bringing any action under this subsection, nothing in this subsection shall prevent the chief law enforcement officer, or an official or agency designated by a State, from exercising the powers conferred on the chief law enforcement officer or such official by the laws of such State to conduct investigations or to administer oaths or affirmations or to compel the attendance of witnesses or the production of documentary and other evidence.

(4) Limitation.—Whenever the Federal Trade Commission has instituted a civil action for violation of this title, no State may, during the pendency of such action, bring an action under this section against any defendant named in the complaint of the Commission for any violation of this title that is alleged in that complaint.

### SECTION 1679I. STATUTE OF LIMITATIONS.

Any action to enforce any liability under this title may be brought before the later of—

(1) the end of the 5-year period beginning on the date of the occurrence of the violation involved; or

(2) in any case in which any credit repair organization has materially and willfully misrepresented any information which—

(A) the credit repair organization is required, by any provision of this title, to disclose to any consumer; and

(B) is material to the establishment of the credit repair organization's liability to the consumer under this title, the end of the 5-year period beginning on the date of the discovery by the consumer of the misrepresentation.

**SECTION 1679J. RELATION TO STATE LAW.**

This title shall not annul, alter, affect, or exempt any person subject to the provisions of this title from complying with any law of any State except to the extent that such law is inconsistent with any provision of this title, and then only to the extent of the inconsistency.

# GLOSSARY

**Abuse of Process**—The improper and malicious use of the criminal or civil process.

**Acceptance**—Acceptance refers to one's consent to the terms of an offer, which consent creates a contract.

**Accord and Satisfaction**—Accord and satisfaction refers to the payment of money, or other thing of value, which is usually less than the amount owed or demanded, in exchange for extinguishment of the debt.

**Accrue**—To occur or come into existence.

**Action at Law**—A judicial proceeding whereby one party prosecutes another for a wrong done.

**Actionable**—Giving rise to a cause of action.

**Actual Damages**—Actual damages are those damages directly referable to the breach or tortious act, and which can be readily proven to have been sustained, and for which the injured party should be compensated as a matter of right.

**Additional Principal Payment**—Additional money included with a loan payment to pay off the amount owed faster thus reducing the amount of interest paid.

**Adhesion Contract**—An adhesion contract is a standardized contract form offered to consumers of goods and services on a "take it or leave it" basis without affording the consumer a realistic opportunity to bargain, and under such conditions that infer coercion.

**Affirmative Defense**—In a pleading, a matter constituting a defense.

# GLOSSARY

**American Arbitration Association (AAA)**—National organization of arbitrators from whose panel arbitrators are selected for labor and civil disputes.

**Annual Fee**—A fee charged by a bank annually for use of a credit card.

**Annual Percentage Rate (APR)**—A yearly rate of interest that includes fees and costs paid to acquire the loan.

**Answer**—In a civil proceeding, the principal pleading on the part of the defendant in response to the plaintiff's complaint.

**Anticipatory Breach of Contract**—A breach committed before the arrival of the actual time of required performance.

**Appearance**—To come into court, personally or through an attorney, after being summoned.

**Arbitration**—The reference of a dispute to an impartial person chosen by the parties to the dispute who agree in advance to abide by the arbitrator's award issued after a hearing at which both parties have an opportunity to be heard.

**Arbitration Clause**—A clause inserted in a contract providing for compulsory arbitration in case of a dispute as to the rights or liabilities under such contract.

**Arbitrator**—A private, disinterested person, chosen by the parties to a disputed question, for the purpose of hearing their contention, and awarding judgment to the prevailing party.

**Arrears**—Payments which are due but not yet paid.

**Asset**—The entirety of a person's property, either real or personal.

**Assignee**—An assignee is a person to whom an assignment is made, also known as a grantee.

**Assignment**—An assignment is the transfer of an interest in a right or property from one party to another.

**Authorized User**—Any person to whom the credit card holder gives permission to use a credit card account.

**Average Daily Balance**—The method by which most credit cards calculate the credit card holder's payment, computed by adding each day's balance and dividing the total by the number of days in a billing cycle.

**Bad Faith**—A willful failure to comply with one's statutory or contractual obligations.

# GLOSSARY

**Bankrupt**—The state or condition of one who is unable to pay his debts as they are, or become, due.

**Bankruptcy**—The legal process governed by federal law designed to assist the debtor in a new financial start while insuring fairness among creditors.

**Bankruptcy Code**—Refers to the Bankruptcy Act of 1978, the federal law which governs bankruptcy actions.

**Bankruptcy Court**—The forum in which most bankruptcy proceedings are conducted.

**Bankruptcy Trustee**—The person, appointed by the bankruptcy judge or selected by the creditors, who takes legal title to the property of the debtor and holds it "in trust" for equitable distribution among the creditors.

**Billing Period**—The number of days used to calculate interest on a loan or credit card.

**Billing Statement**—The monthly bill sent by a credit card issuer to the customer.

**Boilerplate**—Refers to standard language found almost universally in certain documents.

**Breach of Contract**—The failure, without any legal excuse, to perform any promise which forms the whole or the part of a contract.

**Burden of Proof**—The duty of a party to substantiate an allegation or issue to convince the trier of fact as to the truth of their claim.

**Capacity**—Capacity is the legal qualification concerning the ability of one to understand the nature and effects of one's acts.

**Cash Flow**— The difference between cash inflow and cash outflow computed over a certain period of time.

**Cash Inflow**—Cash-based income, such as your salary.

**Cash Outflow**—Expenses, including mortgage payments, living expenses, credit card payments, etc.

**Cause of Action**—The factual basis for bringing a lawsuit.

**Caveat Emptor**—Latin for "let the buyer beware."

**Charge-Off**—A debt deemed uncollectible by the creditor and reported as a bad debt to a credit reporting agency.

# GLOSSARY

**Civil Action**—An action maintained to protect a private civil right as opposed to a criminal action.

**Civil Court**—The court designed to resolve disputes arising under the common law and civil statutes.

**Civil Law**—Law which applies to non-criminal actions.

**Clean Hands Doctrine**—The concept that claimants who seek equitable relief must not themselves have indulged in any impropriety in relation to the transaction upon which relief is sought.

**Closed-End credit**—Credit that requires the borrower to repay the loaned amount without the ability to borrow any of the amount repaid.

**Collateral**—Property which is pledged as additional security for a debt, such as a loan.

**Confession of Judgment**—An admission of a debt by the debtor which may be entered as a judgment without the necessity of a formal legal proceeding.

**Consequential Damages**—Consequential damages are those damages which are caused by an injury, but which are not a necessary result of the injury, and must be specially pleaded and proven in order to be awarded.

**Consideration**—Something of value exchanged between parties to a contract, which is a requirement of a valid contract.

**Consumer Bankruptcy**—A bankruptcy case filed to reduce or eliminate debts that are primarily consumer debts.

**Co-Signer**—A person who signs a promissory note that is also signed by one or more other parties, and for which both parties are responsible for the underlying debt.

**Consumer Credit Counseling Service**—A service that offers counseling to consumers and serves as a intermediary with creditors regarding debt repayment and budget planning.

**Consumer Credit**—Loans for personal or household use as opposed to business or commercial lending.

**Consumer Debts**—Debts incurred for personal needs.

**Contract**—A contract is an agreement between two or more persons which creates an obligation to do or not to do a particular thing.

**Court**—The branch of government responsible for the resolution of disputes arising under the laws of the government.

**Credit**—Money that a lender gives to a borrower on condition of repayment over a certain period.

**Credit History**—A record of an individual's debt payments.

**Credit Insurance**—An insurance policy that pays off credit card debt if the borrower loses his or her job, becomes disabled, or dies.

**Credit Limit**—The maximum amount of charges a cardholder may apply to the account.

**Credit Line**—The maximum amount of money available in an open-end credit arrangement such as a credit card.

**Creditor**—One who is owed money.

**Credit Rating**—A judgment of an individual consumer's ability to repay their debts, based on current and projected income and history of payment of past debts.

**Credit Report**—A credit report refers to the document from a credit reporting agency setting forth a credit rating and pertinent financial data concerning a person or a company, which is used in evaluating the applicant's financial stability.

**Credit Reporting Agency**—A company that issues credit reports on how individual consumers manage their debts and make payments.

**Credit Score**—A number assigned to an individual's credit rating.

**Damages**—In general, damages refers to monetary compensation which the law awards to one who has been injured by the actions of another, such as in the case of tortious conduct or breach of contractual obligations.

**Debt**—Money one person owes another.

**Debt Consolidation Loan**—The replacement of two or more loans with a single loan, usually with a lower monthly payment and a longer repayment period.

**Debt Collector**—Any person or business that regularly collects debts that are owed, or which were originally owed, to another person.

**Defamation**—The publication of an injurious statement about the reputation of another

**Default**—The condition that occurs when a consumer fails to fulfill the obligations set out in a loan.

**Defendant**—In a civil proceeding, the party responding to the complaint.

## GLOSSARY

**Defense**—Opposition to the truth or validity of the plaintiff's claims.

**Delinquent**—Refers to a debt that has not been paid by the payment date or by the end of any grace period.

**Demand for Arbitration**—A unilateral filing of a claim in arbitration based on the filer's contractual or statutory right to do so.

**Disclaimer**—Words or conduct which tend to negate or limit warranty in the sale of goods, which in certain instances must be conspicuous and refer to the specific warranty to be excluded.

**Down Payment**—A partial payment of the purchase price.

**Duress**—Refers to the action of one person which compels another to do something he or she would not otherwise do.

**Equal Credit Opportunity Act**—A federal law that prohibits discrimination in credit on the basis of race, color, religion, national origin, sex, marital status, age, source of income or the exercise of any right under the Consumer Credit Protection Act.

**Equity**—The fair market value of a home less the outstanding mortgage debt, home equity loan or line of credit, and other obligations secured by the home.

**Fair Credit Billing Act**—A federal law passed by Congress in 1975 to help customers resolve billing disputes with card issuers.

**Fair Credit Reporting Act**—A federal law that governs what credit bureaus can report concerning an individual consumer.

**Fair Debt Collection Practices Act**—A federal law that governs debt collection methods.

**Finance Charge**—The charge for using a credit card, including interest costs and other fees.

**Fixed Income**—Income which is unchangeable.

**Forbearance**—A postponement of loan payments, granted by a lender or creditor, for a temporary period of time.

**Foreclosure**—The procedure by which mortgaged property is sold on default of the mortgagor in satisfaction of mortgage debt.

**Fraud**—A false representation of a matter of fact, whether by words or by conduct, by false or misleading allegations, or by concealment of that which should have been disclosed, which deceives and is intended to deceive another, and thereby causes injury to that person.

**Fraudulent Conveyance**—The transfer of property for the purpose of delaying or defrauding creditors.

**Garnish**—To attach the wages or property of an individual.

**Garnishee**—A person who receives notice to hold the assets of another, which are in his or her possession, until such time as a court orders the disposition of the property.

**General Damages**—General damages are those damages directly referable to the breach or tortious act and which can be readily proven to have been sustained, and for which the injured party should be compensated as a matter of right.

**Grace Period**—The interest-free period between the transaction date and the billing date allowed by the credit card issuer provided the credit card holder does not carry a balance on their credit card.

**Guarantor**—One who makes a guaranty.

**Guaranty**—An agreement to perform in the place of another if that person reneges on a promise contained in an underlying agreement.

**Home Equity Credit Line**—A type of revolving credit where the borrower can borrow funds up to an established limit and the funds are secured by the borrower's home.

**Homestead**—The house, outbuilding, and land owned and used as a dwelling by the head of the family.

**Impound**—To place property in the custody of an official.

**In Rem**—Refers to actions that are against property, and concerned with the disposition of that property, rather than against the person.

**Indemnification Clause**—An indemnification clause in a contract refers to the agreement by one party to secure the other party against loss or damage which may occur in the future in connection with performance of the contract.

**Indemnify**—To hold another harmless for loss or damage which has already occurred, or which may occur in the future.

**Injunction**—A judicial remedy either requiring a party to perform an act, or restricting a party from continuing a particular act.

**Injury**—Any damage done to another's person, rights, reputation or property.

# GLOSSARY

**Installment Contract**—An installment contract is one in which the obligation, such as the payment of money, is divided into a series of successive performances over a period of time.

**Interest**—An amount of money paid by a borrower to a lender for the use of the lender's money.

**Interest Rate**—The percentage of a sum of money charged for its use.

**Introductory Rate**—The low rate charged by a lender for an initial period after which the rate increases to the indexed rate or the stated interest rate.

**Judge**—The individual who presides over a court, and whose function it is to determine controversies.

**Judgment**—A judgment is a final determination by a court of law concerning the rights of the parties to a lawsuit.

**Judgment Creditor**—A creditor who has obtained a judgment against a debtor, which judgment may be enforced to obtain payment of the amount due.

**Judgment Debtor**—An individual who owes a sum of money, and against whom a judgment has been awarded for that debt.

**Judgment Proof**—Refers to the status of an individual who does not have the financial resources or assets necessary to satisfy a judgment.

**Late Fee**—A fee charged by a creditor when a payment does not post by the specified due date.

**Legal Capacity**—Referring to the legal capacity to sue, it is the requirement that a person bringing the lawsuit have a sound mind, be of lawful age, and be under no restraint or legal disability.

**Leveraging**—The process of borrowing funds at a low interest rate and investing the funds at a high rate of return.

**Levy**—To seize property in order to satisfy a judgment.

**Liability**—Liability refers to one's obligation to do or refrain from doing something, such as the payment of a debt.

**Libel**—The false and malicious publication, in printed form, for the purpose of defaming another.

**Lien**—A legal claim held by a creditor against an asset to guarantee repayment of a debt.

**Liquidated Damages**—An amount stipulated in a contract as a reasonable estimate of damages to be paid in the event the contract is breached.

**Loan Principal**—The loan principal is the amount of the debt not including interest or any other additions.

**Maker**—As used in commercial law, the individual who executes a note.

**Material Breach**—A material breach refers to a substantial breach of contract which excuses further performance by the innocent party and gives rise to an action for breach of contract by the injured party.

**Maturity Date**—The date upon which a creditor is designated to receive payment of a debt, such as payment of the principal value of a bond to a bondholder by the issuing company or governmental entity.

**Mechanic's Lien**—A claim created by law for the purpose of securing a priority of payment of the price of work performed and materials furnished.

**Mediation**—The act of a third person in intermediating between two contending parties with a view to persuading them to adjust or settle their dispute but without the authority to make a binding decision.

**Minimum Payment**—The minimum amount a credit card holder can pay to keep the account from going into default.

**Minor**—A person who has not yet reached the age of legal competence, which is designated as 18 in most states.

**Monthly Periodic Rate**—The interest rate factor used to calculate the interest charges on a monthly basis, i.e., the yearly rate divided by 12.

**Mortgage**—A written instrument, duly executed and delivered, that creates a lien upon real estate as security for the payment of a specific debt.

**Mutual Agreement**—Mutual agreement refers to the meeting of the minds of the parties to a contract concerning the subject matter of the contract.

**Negotiable Instrument**—A signed writing which contains an unconditional promise to pay a sum of money, either on demand or at a specified time, payable to the order of the bearer.

**Net Income**—Gross income less deductions and exemptions proscribed by law.

**Net Worth**—The difference between one's assets and liabilities.

# GLOSSARY

**Nominal Damages**—A trivial sum of money which is awarded as recognition that a legal injury was sustained, although slight.

**Note**—A writing which promises payment of a debt.

**Novation**—A novation refers to the substitution of a new party and the discharge of an original party to a contract, with the assent of all parties.

**Obligee**—An obligee is one who is entitled to receive a sum of money or performance from the obligor.

**Obligor**—An obligor is one who promises to perform or pay a sum of money under a contract.

**Offeree**—An offeree is the person to whom an offer is made.

**Offeror**—An offeror is the person who makes an offer.

**Open-End Credit**—Revolving credit, such as credit cards, which allow the borrower to make payments and use funds up to an established credit limit.

**Oral Agreement**—An oral agreement is one which is not in writing or not signed by the parties.

**Overdraft Privilege**—Service offered by bank allowing customers to borrow more than the amount on deposit in their bank account.

**Overlimit Fee**—A fee charged by a creditor to the consumer for a balance exceeding the consumer's credit limit.

**Parties**—The disputants.

**Past Due Fee**—A fee charged by a creditor to the consumer when their account is past due.

**Pecuniary**—A term relating to monetary matters.

**Performance**—Performance refers to the completion of one's contractual obligation.

**Principal**—The amount of money owed on a loan excluding interest.

**Rate of Return**—The percentage gain or loss on an investment expressed as a yearly rate.

**Re-Aged Account**—Refers to an account status that is updated to reflect current when the account was delinquent.

**Rate**—Percentage a borrower pays for the use of money.

## GLOSSARY

**Referee's Deed**—A deed given by a referee or other public officer pursuant to a court order for the sale of property.

**Reformation**—An equitable remedy which calls for the rewriting of a contract involving a mutual mistake or fraud.

**Release**—A document signed by one party, releasing claims he or she may have against another party, usually as part of a settlement agreement.

**Repayment Plan**—A plan devised to repay debt.

**Repudiation**—In contract law, refers to the declaration of one of the parties to the contract that he or she will not perform under the contract.

**Rescission**—The cancellation of a contract which returns the parties to the positions they were in before the contract was made.

**Restitution**—The act of making an aggrieved party whole by compensating him or her for any loss or damage sustained.

**Sale**—An agreement to transfer property from the seller to the buyer for a stated sum of money.

**Sale and Leaseback**—An agreement whereby the seller transfers property to the buyer who immediately leases the property back to the seller.

**Satisfaction**—The discharge and release of an obligation.

**Secured Credit Card**—A credit card secured by a savings deposit to ensure payment of the outstanding balance if the credit card holder defaults on payments.

**Secured Loan**—Borrowed money backed by collateral.

**Service of Process**—The delivery of legal court documents, such as a complaint, to the defendant.

**Settlement**—An agreement by the parties to a dispute on a resolution of the claims, usually requiring some mutual action, such as payment of money in consideration of a release of claims.

**Statute of Limitations**—Any law which fixes the time within which parties must take judicial action to enforce rights or thereafter be barred from enforcing them.

**Stay**—A judicial order suspending some action until further court order lifting the stay.

**Stipulation**—An admission or agreement made by parties to a lawsuit concerning the pending matter.

# GLOSSARY

**Subpoena**—A court issued document compelling the appearance of a witness before the court.

**Subpoena Duces Tecum**—A court issued document requiring a witness to produce certain document in his or her possession or control.

**Summons**—A mandate requiring the appearance of the defendant in an action under penalty of having judgment.

**Tangible Property**—Property which is capable of being possessed, whether real or personal.

**Tax**—A sum of money assessed upon one's income, property and purchases, for the purpose of supporting the government.

**Tax Court**—A federal administrative agency which acts as a court for the purposes of determining disputes between individuals and the Internal Revenue Service.

**Tax Bracket**—The range of taxable income by which your income taxes are calculated.

**Tax-Deductible**—An expense or contribution that reduces your taxable income.

**Trial**—The judicial procedure whereby disputes are determined based on the presentation of issues of law and fact. The trier of fact, either the judge or jury, decides issues of fact and the judge decides issues of law.

**Trial Court**—The court of original jurisdiction over a particular matter.

**Truth-In-Lending Act**—A federal law which requires commercial lenders to provide applicants with detailed, accurate and understandable information relating to the cost of credit, so as to permit the borrower to make an informed decision.

**Unconscionable**—Refers to a bargain so one-sided as to amount to an absence of meaningful choice on the part of one of the parties, together with terms which are unreasonably favorable to the other party.

**Undue Influence**—The exertion of improper influence upon another for the purpose of destroying that person's free will in carrying out a particular act, such as entering into a contract.

**Unsecured Credit**—Credit extended without collateral.

**Unsecured Debt**—Debt not guaranteed by the pledge of collateral, e.g. a credit card.

**Unsecured Loan**—An advance of money that is not secured by collateral.

**Usurious Contract**—A contract that imposes interest at a rate which exceeds the legally permissible rate.

**Usury**—An excessive rate of interest above the maximum permissible rate established by the state legislature.

**Vitiate**—To make void.

**Void**—Having no legal force or binding effect.

**Voidable**—Capable of being rendered void and unenforceable.

**Voluntary Arbitration**—Arbitration which occurs by mutual and free consent of the parties.

# BIBLIOGRAPHY AND ADDITIONAL READING

Black Law Dictionary, Fifth Edition. St. Paul, MN: West Publishing Company, 1979.

Consumer Sentinel (Date Visited: September 2006) <http://www.consumer.gov/sentinel/>.

Equifax (Date Visited: September 2006) <http://www.equifax.com/>.

Experian (Date Visited: September 2006) <http://www.experian.com/>.

Federal Trade Commission (Date Visited: September 2006) <http://www.ftc/gov/>.

Internal Revenue Service (Date Visited: September 2006) <http://www.irs.ustreas.gov>.

TransUnion (Date Visited: September 2006) <http://www.transunion.com/>.